The Boys of Cortlandt
& The Iron Men of Croton

Peter J. Gorton

RPSS Publishing - Buffalo, New York

publisher@rockpapersafetyscissors.com

ISBN: 978-1-7349144-4-3
Printed in the United States of America

10 9 8 7 6 5 4 3 2 1

RPSS Publishing - Buffalo, New York

I dedicate this book to my mom and dad;

John and Blanche Gorton;

my brothers John and Robert Gorton;

my daughter Karlee Lewis and my son Dustin Gorton;

my late wife Susan (Lewis) Gorton;

to my friendship with Craig Telfer and Barry Booker;

and most importantly to the Bailey family and all its

branches past and present.

Mr. Cruger

Tellers Pt. or C
inderhills Grape Vineya

Prologue

Life is funny with its twists and turns; decisions are made, and the journey goes on—no way to tell what would have become of one's life if different choices were selected. There is no way to tell, no way of knowing the outcome. And so your selections determine what your life will be. Or maybe there is some certain destiny to it all. Of course, who knows that either.

It's like when you stand in an open doorway on a rainy summer day gazing out with a melancholy mood thinking of life gone by and the choices you made and where you wound up. Straining to pretend that if you chose a different path, the outcome would be x and not y. Then, your eyes catch a beautiful flower in the foreground that is partially obscuring a magnificently beautiful plant in full bloom in the background. Your eyes go back and forth, focusing on the flower and the plant until your melancholy mood returns, and you lose focus on both. You turn and walk away from the door and back to life, and the journey continues.

When you are young, you look at your parents and grandparents, and you view life as idyllic—as if the life you know and the people you love will go on forever. As your grandparents pass away and then your parents, you realize that your kids will lose you too; that life is short and precious. When you look back at your ancestors long ago, their lives are nothing more than momentary events. They are a moment in time for you, as your life, if it's ever remembered, will also be.

But things have a habit of repeating themselves. Maybe it's part of the universe; it seems to happen too often to be a coincidence. Some have defined this as Historic Recurrence or the repetition of patterns. It has its own doctrine—the Doctrine of Eternal Recurrence: "The theory that existence recurs in an infinite cycle as energy and matter transform over time." Nietzsche connected this concept to many things. Perhaps when it comes to personality, human behavior, and family, the theory can be tied to ancestry, to heredity. But does it override the changing culture, or does culture also repeat? The organization known as Ancestry says, "historically, surnames evolved as a way to sort people into groups—by occupation, place of origin, clan affiliation, patronage, parentage, adoption, and even physical characteristics (like red hair)."

Perhaps heredity speaks through many generations using surnames as a marker for the eternal recurrence.

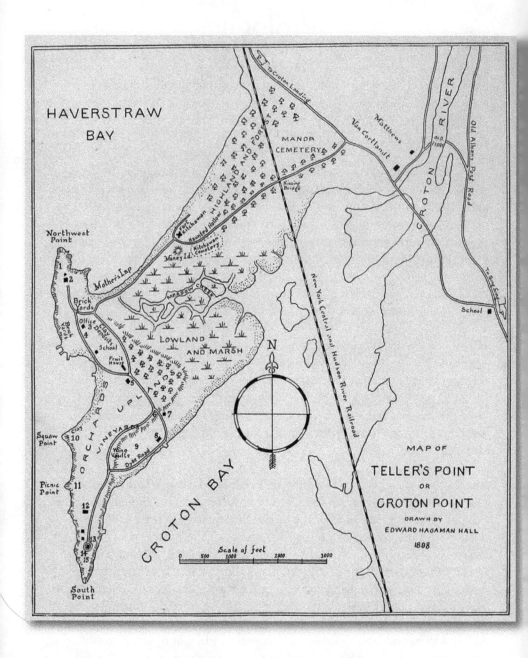

MAP OF

TELLER'S POINT

OR

CROTON POINT

DRAWN BY

EDWARD HAGAMAN HALL

1898

HAVERSTRAW BAY

Northwest Point

Mother's Lap

Brick Yards

Squaw Point

Picnic Point

South Point

CROTON BAY

MEADOW CREEK

LOWLAND AND MARSH

ORCHARDS UPLAND VINEYARDS

Wine Vaults

Dyke Road

Clay

Office

Clay Deposits

School

Fruit House

HIGHLAND AND FOREST

Fort Kitchawan

Haunted Hollow

Kitchawan Cemetery

Money Id.

MANOR CEMETERY

Kissing Bridge

To Croton Landing

Van Cortlandt

Matthews

CROTON RIVER

Old Albany Post Road

To Sing Sing

School

New York Central and Hudson River Railroad

N

Scale of feet

0   500   1000   2000   3000

CHAPTER 1
The Match

1968–1973

"Hey, where is Nick? The rest of the team is on the bench, but I don't see Nick," Scott said as he hustled into the gym with his girlfriend, Tracy, and sat beside the guys assembled at the top of the bleachers to watch the rival wrestling match with Peekskill. The gym was packed because wrestling was almost as popular as basketball in their school in the 1970s. The team was good, and this was the big rival match. Nick was scheduled to wrestle Peekskill's star wrestler—someone no one liked in school. The kid from Peekskill was an egotistical guy who had been messing with the girls in their school, which was frowned upon. This was a big test for Nick, who was a little-known wrestler in Section One wrestling. He was a sophomore and was only introduced to the sport of wrestling a year earlier. His older friends from the neighborhood who were on the team suggested Nick try out. The senior on the team in his 132-pound weight class was a friend who Nick knew from his neighborhood. He was hurt, so Nick was brought up from junior varsity to varsity after he won the wrestle-offs to get the spot. Before each match, he had to wrestle-off other kids on his team at his weight vying for this chance. It was very competitive in a school this big. In a big school in this era, competition was tough, and it was not uncommon to have multiple kids in certain weight classes. The rule was that anyone could challenge you to a wrestle-off, and the winner would wrestle the next match and those after until he lost a wrestle-off. Nick typically had to wrestle off someone before each match to retain the spot. Prior to the Peekskill match, Nick had already had two previous varsity matches that he won. At that time, in the late 1960s and early 1970s, the most competition on any wrestling team and among other schools was typically in the weight classes ranging from 125 to 165 pounds. Those were the weights that the majority of boys fell in high school—more kids, more competition.

Nick had not yet developed a rep in the wrestling community because he had mostly been on JV and was really new to the sport. Besides being smart and athletic, Nick was always a student of anything he did. Nick was probably good enough to beat the senior on varsity at his weight, but because he was a friend and a senior, Nick figured he could wait till next year for varsity. That was typical Nick. The injury to his friend changed all that and changed Nick's future. Everyone in wrestling knew who the best wrestlers were on each team, and often teams would position their wrestlers around who they were going to meet in each weight class. Wrestling matches were broken up by weight classes. To wrestle a certain weight class, you had to be that weight or less. So, you could be 140 and wrestle in the 160-weight class, but you could not be 160 and wrestle in the 140-weight class—or 155 for that matter. This made for some difficult times "making weight" and some interesting methods to accomplish it. Nick had heard that Peekskill knew an unknown JV wrestler was in the 132 class, and they positioned their star in that class to avoid one of Nick's teammates, who was a superior wrestler. This only made Nick more focused.

Everyone in school knew who Nick would be wrestling from Peekskill, and the pressure was intense. On top of that, he was wrestling an established guy—a guy with a rep—one of the best wrestlers in the county. All week long, people came up to Nick in the gym, in the cafeteria, in the halls between classes and told him it was his duty to beat this kid—for the school's honor. It had developed into a mini-event.

Wrestling is a physically and mentally grueling sport, a uniquely individual sport. Sure, there is the team, but the team only accumulates points based on individual matches. It's you and another human in a small circle. No one else, no teammates; it's all you—a blend of strength, stamina, physical and mental toughness, and will. The best wrestlers have these qualities and more. The best all have the will to win, the training to do it, and the mental strength to succeed. But they also have something else. When you get to the highest level, everyone is good. Everyone is trained. Everyone has the will. But the best of the best in wrestling is something that is hard to define. There is this slight nuance that makes the difference between the very good and the very best. Perhaps it's best described as the need to win above all without the fear of losing. The very best don't play not to lose. Perhaps only those who have reached that level in sport or business or life understand this nuance. At the very top levels of high school and collegiate wrestling—or the Olympics, for that matter—it comes down to mentality. It was common knowledge that the very best wrestlers were a little "crazy." Truly different individuals succeed in this sport. Like boxing, it's physically and mentally draining. Wrestlers exert so much isometric force in a short period of time, and pre-match rituals are as much for preparing the body as they are a metal exercise to overcome the sport's unique stress. There is a special kind of butterflies in the stomach before each match. Every match is a unique six minutes of desire, and wrestlers face that desire every time they step on the mat. The desire to be the best, to win, is put to the test every match, and during each match, you learn a little more about yourself. It's a truly unique sport with only a few equals. It's you and the other guy, each time in a circle, and no one else can wrestle for you but you.

In the early 1970s, high school wrestling matches consisted of three consecutive two-minute time periods—six minutes of mental and physical hell where only the very best excelled. If the score is tied at the end of the third period, there is a one-minute overtime period, and if necessary, 30-second tiebreakers. Wrestling is full out kinetic energy of short, quick movements and isometric force; it's six minutes of full out, extreme mental and physical action. The best require an extreme amount of will to succeed—reaching deeper and farther than most will reach. There were twelve distinct weight classes in high school men's freestyle wrestling in the 1970s, starting at the 98-pound division up to the 215-pound division, and sometimes they added an unlimited weight class.

Scott did not usually come to wrestling matches because after the soccer season, he was always busy working. But he knew this was a special match. "Nick's in the back room of the gym doing his pre-warmup thing," one of the guys said to Scott. Scott said, "So he made weight then. Man, he was in the showers all day with the rubber suit trying to get down to weight. I don't get these wrestlers and the losing weight thing." But something was different today. Nick was usually on the bench by this time before his match, and he was nowhere in sight.

Nick cracked the door open slightly from the work-out room and peered out at a completely full gym. The match had already started, and the early weight classes were wrestling. He looked immediately at the big scoreboard on the gym wall opposite the mat and quickly scanned to see what weight class was wrestling so he could judge how long it would be before his match. His gaze went from the scoreboard to the gym floor. He looked at the mat in the middle of two rows of chairs full of his teammates and the opposing team on either side of the mat. He glanced directly at his opponent to gauge his demeanor and knew instantly that this kid was a little overconfident. Sometimes matches were won at the weigh-in. In high school, once the other team arrived, they would get undressed and stand in parallel lines by weight to weigh-in; one by one, they would get on the scale with the referee confirming if weight was made or not. A lot of pre-match body language would take place trying to psyche out the other guy. Unlike today, in the early 1970s, very little smack talking occurred and was certainly not common; it was more frowned upon then.

Nick's eyes wandered up to the bleachers, and he saw his brother sitting in the middle of the stands. He never told his brother, but he appreciated that he showed up to almost every home match and even some away matches. Nick's mom and dad never came to wrestling. His mom had shown up to a match when Nick first started wrestling and could not take it. She told Nick that she could not sit and watch her baby in that grueling sport. The only other time they showed up was later in Nick's wrestling career at the end of the Divisional Tournament, just in time to see him stand on the podium and get a medal. Nick's gaze moved to the top rows, where he knew his friends would be sitting. Just as he caught sight of some of his friends, he noticed Scott and his girlfriend rush in to sit down. Scott had said he was coming, but Nick wasn't sure because Scott rarely came to matches. But he was late as always. Scott was usually late because he was always hustling from one appointment or work or party to the next. Because he was such a gregarious personality, he was usually involved and thus always late leaving. Nick understood this about Scott, and thus it never bothered him. Others, however, often got mad when Scott did not show at the appointed time because they did not understand Scott or his personality and some were just jealous.

Sitting at the end of the bench was Nick's girlfriend, Eve: a beautiful girl with long brown hair and big, beautiful, warm brown eyes. They started dating when Nick was sixteen, and she was fourteen, but they had met earlier. Nick remembers seeing her the first time when they were both little, and his oldest brother took him fishing in a small cement pond next to the street Eve lived on. It was more of a cement holding pond that channeled the water down the slope toward Oregon Road, but Nick's older brother knew it would be full of "Sunnies" (Sunfish) that would bite on anything. This may have been the first time Nick had ever been freshwater fishing, but he remembers these two bratty pretty girls asking them what they were doing because they were across this small pond on the street where she lived. Nick and Eve lived about ten minutes' walk-in separate neighborhoods separated by what was commonly referred to as the Jewish colony. It got this name because it was a small community of bungalow-type houses with a small man-made lake, paddleball court, and gathering area. Most of the people who lived in these houses came for the summer from the Jewish neighborhoods of New York City, and this was their summer get-away "upstate" in the "country." This was the center of Nick's life growing up: fishing in the lake, playing endless games of ice hockey with the neighborhood boys, and playing stickball and handball on the paddleball court. This is also the place where Nick kissed Eve for the first time behind the paddleball court. Nick loved his girlfriend. The type of love that could last a lifetime but seldom gets the opportunity. She was beautiful, kind, loving, and Nick learned a great deal about being a good person from her. She smoothed out his raging masculinity as good women do for good men.

The gym was packed, and Nick was super nervous. He was always nervous before a match, but this was worse than usual because of the pressure all his classmates had put on him. He shut the door to the scene and picked up a jump rope. As he went through his pre-match ritual of jumping rope, listening to the ratta-tat of the rope hitting the floor with each pass, he began to wonder why he put himself through this. His stomach felt like it was going to come through his mouth, and he felt like he wanted to jump out of his skin. No matter how many matches and how many wins, all good wrestlers were nervous before a match, and Nick was a good wrestler, a very good wrestler. He thought, "Man, I could be up there with my friends laughing and having fun with no cares instead of walking out on that mat and into the circle with the whole gym focused on me." Even though he knew that when the match started, all that would go away, he still hated this part, and this time was so much worse.

The more he jumped rope, the more he began to focus on the match, and he started to think about how he would beat this guy. He knew it would be an intense match that would require him to make no mistakes—none. He was actually surprised when he saw the kid during the weigh-in. He was smaller and obviously did not have to lose weight to make this class, whereas Nick was normally about 145-155 during football and was skinny at that. Nick had to work hard to get down to this weight class of 132, and he was solid muscle and not an ounce of fat with ripped stomach muscles. In this era of early 1970 sports, it was very rare for coaches to spend time preparing their kids for a specific opponent. There were no films to study or tendencies to review—at least not at this level, and most high school coaches were really just history or science or gym teachers. Most matches started with limited knowledge of your opponent unless the guy was one of the elites that people knew. There were also none of the trainers or specialty coaches that exist today. Nick came by his physicality and mental acuity on his own as a natural outcome of his own training and heredity, and he had no conscious knowledge of it. It's not that he was smarter than the other wrestlers, although he probably was smarter than many. It was that he had the ability to focus completely on a task and had the mental toughness to push beyond. He had superior brain health, which gave him an edge in speed, reaction time, attention, visual screening ability, and processing speed.

"Wow," one of the guys who comes to all the matches said. "Nick is usually on the bench for the early matches—it's part of the team thing. He must be nervous about the match." Before each match begins, the team runs out of the gym in the order of their weight class in their full uniform, warmup gear/school colors, and runs around the outer circle of the mat to their side of the mat. A series of chairs are set up along each sideline so that both teams face each other across the mat. Since this was a home match, the other team had already come in, and we're sitting in their seats. Nick had come out with the team and run the ritual circle around the mat to their seats. But right away, he got up and left for the back warmup area. He needed to be alone. He needed to focus, and he wanted to make an entrance on this guy as a bit of mystery. Nick was always thinking, always had a plan. He knew the guy knew little about him, and he could tell during the weigh-in that the guy was somewhat surprised at Nick's size and muscle. Nick knew this kid had heard he was wrestling an unknown sophomore, as the rumors drifted between the schools for this event. So even though the guy was acting self-assured during the weigh-in, Nick caught a slight look telling him that his physical appearance must have surprised his opponent, who was thinking he was facing a skinny sophomore. Coming out of the backroom late would build upon this guy's doubts and delay the stare-down that always occurred across the mat at your opponent.

Nick's match was about to start, and the guys were wondering where he was. Is he hurt? Is he sick? Just then, the door to the warmup room burst open, and in runs Nick. He goes to the edge of the mat. His coach says something to him, and the strongest guy on the team—a guy with arms the size of tree trunks who wrestles three weight classes above Nick—is standing there, and he slaps Nick hard across the face. Scott and his girlfriend glance at each other with this "holy shit" look, and then at the rest of the guys, and both say in unison,

"Oh my God." The guy who regularly attends the matches smiles and replied that that's part of Nick's pre-match ritual: "I asked him about it, and he told me he wants to get the first contact out right away, so he is ready for the match, and he thinks it psyches out his opponent." Scott said, "Really, you think? Yeah, that sounds like Nick. Always thinking, Nick is."

As they came to the center circle, both Nick and the guy from Peekskill are staring at one another, and they shake hands, and just as quickly, the match starts in the standing position as the shriek of the ref's whistle sounds. They both circle the inner mat sizing each other up; Nick the bigger, stronger looking guy and his opponent the slighter, quicker looking one even though they are both in the same weight class. True to Nick, he had done some pre-match research on his opponent. He knew this guy's signature move was a quick single-leg takedown and that he relied on his quickness. Just as Nick was reminding himself to be ready, the guy shoots in and gets in deep on his right leg. Just as quickly, Nick moves to the side while slipping in a wizard, leans hard on the guy's shoulder, and comes back out to the neutral position—no points awarded. Nick realizes he was lucky there. He would have to be quick to counter this guy. The wizard relies on speed, balance, strength, and physics, but it does not always work when your opponent gets in deep on a leg. All thoughts of nervousness gone, Nick thinks how impressed he is with the guy's quickness; he's going to have to really be quick himself as he hears his friend Mike (his teammate and the best guy on the team a weight class above) yell just that across the mat. This is a better opponent than he has wrestled before. Although Nick was more muscular than this opponent, that was not always the case. Many times, Nick had faced stronger opponents. This was a tough sport, very tough. Despite his physicality, Nick was also very quick because without knowing it, his training for other sports and his daily work enhanced his quick-twitch muscles, the muscle fibers responsible for initiating the explosive speed and power movements that served Nick well. He also had genetics for above-average reflexes that some athletes possess. His brain health also gave him the ability to process things quickly and act on them.

All through the first period, it was the same quick shoot in for a single leg takedown and a quick counter wizard by Nick. Nick knew he was wearing his opponent down with every wizard as he was purposefully leaning in hard on his shoulder joint with his weight and strength and making him work hard to come back out front. He had set him up. He realized that this was the only move this guy had; he relied on it as it probably beat 90% of the kids this guy had wrestled. On the fourth attempt, as he shot for a quick single-leg, Nick put the wizard in but did not wizard out to the neutral position. Instead, he stepped over the top and gained the advantage for two points. He immediately sensed some doubt and hesitation in the guy's movements now. The setup had worked, and now he was in this guy's head. He rode him out for the remainder of the period by just sheer strength and will. He was imparting his will on this guy, and it took all of Nick's strength and quickness to do it.

As his friends watched the match drag on, they could see Nick take control. Typical of Nick's style, he was a defensive counter attacker aggressively capitalizing on his opponents' mistakes or setting them up for a later move. When he wrestled lesser opponents or when he took control, he became more aggressive and offensive. But not with this guy. Too much was riding on this match to get caught trying to be too aggressive. It's not uncommon for a better wrestler to get what's known in wrestling as "getting Caught" meaning they get overconfident, and the opponent catches them in a move. Nick would be happy to just beat this guy by a point.

In the second period, Nick won the coin flip and chose the down position. He immediately escaped and was now leading the match by three to zero. When given a choice, Nick always chose down in the second period because he figured he had more energy needed for escape moves, and his opponent would be more tired in the third period when it became his turn to be down. The rest of the period was attack by his opponent and counter by Nick. Nick tried to step over for a takedown but with no success, and his opponent tried to change up some takedown moves, but Nick always countered. As the third period started, the two were dripping wet in sweat. Nick started this period in the up position and spent the first minute still in control. Then his opponent escaped for one point, and the match was 3-1 in Nick's favor; a simple takedown by his opponent would tie the match, and his opponent was dangerously good. Again, the single-leg shot and Nick's counter—back and forth, not even thinking about it anymore. The movements were reflexes that have become second nature through many hours of practice. The ref warns Nick that he needs to be more offensive, or he will risk being deducted a point for "stalling." Nick quickly calculates the time left and figures that even if the ref gives his opponent a point, he will still be up by a point. However, instead of taking a chance, he decides instead to move in for a halfhearted takedown that he knows will be countered but not put him in danger while at the same time make it look like he has taken some offense and taking the ref's chance of calling stalling to go away.

As time begins to wind down quickly, his opponent starts to get desperate and picks up the pace. Nick goes on full out defense because he respects this guy's ability and knows his desperation. His team needs the victory to win the dual meet. In desperation, the guy shoots in badly, totally out of any offensive position, and holds onto Nick's legs, tightly gripping as Nick leans his whole body on top and the time slips away. The buzzer sounds. The match is over; the stands go nuts, and the bench runs over to the edge of the mat to greet Nick. They all knew how big this match was. As the opponents shake hands, the ref raises Nick's hand as the winner, and Nick turns to walk away. As he turns, he sees his opponent's head droop, and he feels a slight pity. Just when he reaches the edge of the mat and before reaching his teammates who are all standing waiting to congratulate him, Nick turns to look back and sees his opponent kneeling on the mat, head down and hands covering his face while his coach tries to console him. This was a debilitating match; the cocky kid was beaten by an unknown. Not just beaten but controlled, and he knew it.

Nick was a cerebral wrestler; he typically outthought his opponent and used whatever he could to get an edge. Although Nick was a very good athlete, he was not necessarily a natural. He used his intellect, training, and strength to augment his athletic ability. Sometimes he would distract his opponent by saying something to him and then strike while the guy was giving an answer. There was no talking in this match after the first couple of minutes when the Peekskill wrestler played the intimidation game of cockily suggesting he would kill Nick. He did not know Nick; he did not know that this kind of intimidation worked oppositely on Nick. After the guy said that to Nick, Nick was determined to beat this guy. When the match was over, Nick felt that slight pity as he left the guy crying on the mat. The kid was devastated at the loss—his first of the year at the hands of a no-name sophomore who had dominated him. This guy was never the same wrestler after this match. He knew he was dominated by Nick despite the close score, and his confidence was shot. Later in the season, this guy was not even ranked during tournament time and had dropped down a weight class. Wrestling typically shows no compassion. The good wrestlers quickly pick themselves up, learn from the loss, and return to practice and continue to wrestle. This guy had the need to win but could not handle this loss. But the match also showed why although Nick was a superior wrestler, he would never be the best. His fear of losing prevented it.

CHAPTER 2
Cortlandt and the Boys

My name is Jedidiah—a biblical name that traces back to an ancestor long ago. I was assigned this case, which was supposed to be my last case because I am a master historian and familiar with the geographic and historical record of Cortlandt. My main task was that of assembling portions of the detailed history for the process, adding the background that gives substance to the otherwise un-sequenced events the process spits out. The process requires trained historians with extensive knowledge of genealogy and DNA database research. It's not important to go into detail about the process here only to explain that it was designed for the purpose of creating an extensive ancestral, genealogical and historical record of an individual's makeup through a study of specific parts of the familial tradition .

I have direct ancestors that lived in Cortlandt, one of whom fought in a famous Revolutionary War battle and later settled there. The head of the department said, "It was thought as the icing on the cake of a long, illustrious career for me to focus on a case from the area of my ancestors." What I did not know, but would come to find out, was that my own ancestral history weaved through that of the boys here and there through time. Totally unexpectedly, the connection jumped out of the past and into the present as I began my research of Cortlandt and the boys. My own genealogy and DNA confirmed that I was almost 80% African, including Nigerian, West African, and Kenyan, with some connections from the Maasai tribe—a proud people known for their fighting prowess and warriors. But I also have 21% British and Irish ancestry.

I became very focused as the past began to play out before me and the boys' spirits and ancestral history became real— as if I were right there in real-time with my ancestors who lived at that time. Their lives spilled out in individual events. Each unique event provided substance to the individual family members' physical appearance captured in photographs and film and offered the required insight into the nature of their souls. The process was a powerful tool when combined with the historical context of the subjects and the places they lived. My job was to add the context and the historical surrounding to the somewhat mundane details that were laid out from the process. I quickly became engrossed in my work, becoming one with the detail, and found myself in their time almost like an unseen observer. I was shocked when aspects and people from my own history popped out.

Before I put the final story together for the process, I took a long kayak trip, which served to provide me with much needed mental clarity and physical exhaustion. As I was about to exit my truck after just backing into a spot, a woman caught my eye, but I was not sure why. She had pulled into the large parking lot a good distance away just after I did, and I watched as she got out of her vehicle and removed a fishing pole and other fishing gear from the rear of her vehicle. Normally I would jump right out of my truck because I was in a hurry to get on the water and clear my mind; however, for some reason, I became focused on this woman. After watching her for what seemed like 5 minutes, I finally got out of my pick-up truck and began unpacking my kayak. I found myself still focused on her while I undid the straps. She was about 500 yards away—far enough that I could make out her form but not close enough to actually discern her features. Perhaps that added to her allure. It was early morning, and I guess I found it interesting that this woman would pull up by herself to fish. At first, I thought maybe she was there to kayak, and I would need to hurry to get to the kayak launch so as not to hold her up. But when she opened the back of her SUV, she pulled out fishing gear. I could see enough to notice that she was petite, maybe 5'3", and was wearing a baseball cap and had her hair in a ponytail. I could not quite make out her appearance because the distance was too far for my old eyes to quite make out, though I strained to do so. I had this desire to go over and make small talk. As the thought struck me, I wondered why. Was it just sexist curiosity about why a young, petite girl would be fishing by herself? My mind wandered as to why. Perhaps she had grown up fishing with her dad, and this was a special treat to go out by herself to fish. That thought restrained my desire to speak to her, and I grabbed my kayak and headed for the launch, which was a distance from where she had chosen to fish. I figured she chose to come alone, and the last thing she was looking for was some guy approaching her to make small talk. When I entered the water in my kayak, I lost thought of her as I paddled downstream in the other direction at a steady, hard pace. I was intent on clearing my head and getting in a good workout.

I finished my kayak trip and was pulling hard for the dock. As I did, I suddenly realized the woman was still there fishing. Suddenly intrigued by this woman again, I decided to paddle up past her on the opposite side of the water far enough upstream past her fishing spot with the thought that I would float down on her side and make that small talk. As I turned about 500 yards above her, I once again realized that my first instinct was still true. She was there to be on her own and did not need an interruption. Nor did she need me disturbing the fish with my paddles. I paddled down along the opposite shore again, only stopping briefly to admire some beautiful tulips growing wild along the bank in this early spring morning. I focused on one particular tulip with its yellow petals, or tepals, and the inner orange/purple female and male parts— the pistil and stigma—in the middle. As I focused on these colors, my eye wandered down to the bulbs protruding from the soil as they lapped up some water along the water's edge. It crossed my mind that probably sometime in the past, a house was located on this property that was now just a bank along a walking trail. Or perhaps someone had bulldozed the land above, and these tulip bulbs were pushed over the edge and spilled down the bank toward the water. Whatever had happened, I concluded, they seemed uniquely out of place along an otherwise colorless bank of rock, bush, and weeds just up from the mouth of the Croton River. This was the location of a relatively new kayak-only launch put in so that the kayakers had their own spot far enough away to avoid the boat launch that was farther down where the Croton emptied into the magnificent Hudson River.

I headed toward the kayak launch once again, concluding I would not bother this woman. As I pulled myself back onto the launch from the water, I looked over and saw her sitting on a bench along the water, intensely working on something with her line. Though she was facing me, I was still not close enough to get a clear view of her features. My curiosity intensified as I wiped away some sweat and subsequent tears that were blurring my vision. I watched her small frame straining, and just as her face was close to coming into focus, she spun on her seat, facing away from me. As I got my gear and kayak back on the truck, latching the boat for my ride home, I noticed she was packing her fishing gear, and I thought that she had not stayed there long to fish. As I sat again in my truck, my focus was once again on her. Then a puff of smoke spiraled away from her mouth, blurring her features more. I put my truck in gear and headed home to write history.

The years spanned the late 1960s and early 1970s, and the location was an area 40–60 miles north of New York City in the Hudson River Valley, Hudson Highlands, and surrounding areas. The boys grew up in Cortlandt and attended a large school district outside Peekskill, New York. Theirs was the middle of the baby boom generation, and enrollment in their school district was so big that it required split sessions and eventually the construction of a new school.

Even though they lived less than two miles apart along Oregon Road, no one is sure when the boys' paths first crossed. Nick McCarthy had attended St. Columbanus Catholic Elementary School and lived off Varian Road in the neighborhood known as Evergreen Knolls. Scott Croft attended Van Cortlandt Elementary and lived off Oregon Road on Stevenson Avenue, closer to the City of Peekskill. The two could not recall when they first met. It may have been at CYO basketball or when they both played little league baseball together, or it may have been when Nick transferred to Scott's middle school in 7th grade. Their bonds obviously started to take hold by freshman year in high school when they both played on the Junior Varsity soccer team.

All anyone knows is that by 10th and 11th grades, they were best friends—as close or closer than brothers. They were similar in appearance and strongly male, both attractive, Scott more so than Nick, who was more ruggedly handsome. The combination of their physical appearance coupled with their confidence and at ease presence made them natural leaders, but not leaders in the sense that they ran for some office in school or tried to tell others what to do. They were just the type of guys who others were naturally drawn to; they did not put forth any effort to accomplish this and had no preconceived notion of superiority. They really were totally unaware, oblivious to how they were perceived by others. They were just well-adapted boys living their lives. They were positive guys but not overtly so, self-assured but also regularly self-effacing, with a self-aware and humble style that could endear them to the people they came in contact with. They were pure and authentic in every interaction.

Oh, sure, they were not perfect by any means, and they certainly had their share of flaws. Their hard work ethic was not one of them as they both had a strong work ethic instilled by their families and perhaps ancestry. Although different, they both had these qualities. Scott was more outgoing and gregarious with reddish-brown hair, and Nick was more confidently shy with brown hair with reddish highlights. Nick's outward shyness hid his inner confidence, but he never failed to take command when situations arose. The boys oozed masculinity but yet at times were vulnerable. Their kind of masculinity, at least at that time in America, naturally attracted people who were drawn to their fun and self-assured positive attitudes, both playful and strongly male. But this also attracted bullies—guys who were challenged by their presence.

This typically resulted in some confrontations. As much as they always chose to avoid fights, they did not back down and would always protect their honor and the honor of their friends—and of course, of the women who were part of their lives. This was part of their code; it was part of their DNA. One of their flaws was that they were prideful guys. It was a major part of their personalities. Biology dictated who they were and culture and tradition molded how they acted. Biologically very masculine males, their family culture, heredity, and traditions molded who they were while the changing societal norms influenced their actions. Nick and Scott always thought of and treated women as equals, capable of certainly doing anything they could do mentally and only differ in their physicality. The boys were instinctively attracted to women as their biology dictated. There was no changing this as you could not change the biological instincts of others. Their values and tradition always ruled their behavior. Were they perfect? By no means and in many ways.

Scott was confident, strong, friendly, and funny. Nick was exactly the same, only with a shy and a more self-reflective nature, not necessarily brooding but highly thoughtful at times. Nick's often genuine self-effacing and humble style made him as approachable to others as Scott's gregarious nature made him. Nick was often deep in thought, which Scott always playfully teased him about. Nick's aggressive side was always on display when he played sports, especially hockey or football. Confidently shy is really the best way to explain him. Not afraid to voice an opinion but often shy about it. As a boy, Nick was more shy than aggressive—sort of like a newborn colt just getting the feeling of the power and strength that lies within as it takes its first prance around the paddock. By the time he and Scott were friends, his confidence was more mature. When events overtook his thinking, such as in the middle of an athletic event or when challenged, his aggression was always asserted. He would find himself in the middle of a fight, for example, later realizing he did not know why he jumped in; it was just instinctive, usually to support friends or to protect someone's honor or to face down the bully. Otherwise, he would prefer to have walked away for the fear he might hurt himself or, worse, someone else.

There was a bond between these two. They trusted each other. True friendship between boys and men who went through intense situations together whether in sports or war or in day to day survival from one day to the next. Or, perhaps there was more to it.

This was an age when true honest masculinity was not viewed as a detriment or a bad thing, and the honor it brought them, and their friends, was always rewarded and not ridiculed or deemed toxic, for they were the antithesis of bullies, who in reality are not masculine at all. The boys' masculinity honored their gender and was as much a part of them as anything else.

The era and the place they grew up combined to form a perfect, somewhat idyllic backdrop to their lives and were very much a major influence in their personalities. In a huge way, they were lucky. They grew up in the outskirts of the City of Peekskill in the Town of Cortlandt in what was really more ruggedly rural than suburban. Cortlandt is in the northwestern corner of Westchester County, New York, and is roughly bounded by the Hudson River to the west, by Putnam County to the north, the Town of Yorktown to the east, and by the Towns of New Castle and Ossining to the south. It's approximately forty square miles. The topography is very hilly, with steep slopes and valleys. This rural-like area consists of wooded hills and rugged terrain with steep slopes leading to fairly flat fields. The many streams and wetlands make up part of the Hudson River watershed, and the area contains large public water reservoirs. The Hudson River Valley and Hudson Highlands dominate the magnificent, intense beauty of the area. Among this beauty were numerous residential neighborhoods hidden in among the hills and valleys.

Cortlandt at that time was inhabited by a combination of old families and newer families that arrived at various times and especially after the end of World War II. Some of the older families dated back well before the revolutionary war, which was fought in this area. During the late 1950s and early 1960s, many of the newer families were post-WWII transplants from the New York City metropolitan area, its five boroughs, and the small cities that surrounded it. Both Nick's and Scott's parents had moved here after the war to raise their families. Nick's parents moved from Yonkers into a brand-new neighborhood that was full of young families in the post-war era. It was the Evergreen Knolls neighborhood that rose from the bottom of Oregon Road along Varian Road and up a steep hill and around a loop at the top of the hill. The brochure that sold the neighborhood was right out of a 1950s ad campaign—a new neighborhood in the country with evergreens, dogwood trees, and half-acre lots. You could choose from any of three styles of three- or four-bedroom houses starting around $20,000.

The topography of the neighborhood provided clear, distinct sections referred to casually by the inhabitants as the bottom of the hill, the middle of the hill, and the top of the hill. Nick's family was from the middle of the hill, and most of his friends were kids from houses around his or from the other neighborhoods that ran adjacent to the back of their yards. Later he developed deep friendships with kids from the other sections of the neighborhood. Often they would play rival neighborhoods in pick-up hockey and tackle football games that would last hours. Back then, there were no adults involved in running these games—these were pick-up games organized and played by the kids. What Scott and Nick did not know was that their family roots did go back to the early days of Cortlandt. Perhaps it was just a coincidence that they wound up living in the area of their ancestors. None of that entered their minds. They had little time or care for history; they were young men living their lives in the present.

Most of the inhabitants of Cortlandt at that time were honest, hardworking people who grew up with the puritan work ethic either because their forefathers settled this part of America and fought the American Revolution on these grounds, or they were the descendants of immigrants who came over in the various waves from the mid-1800s through the 1930s. Some were ancestors of slaves. Regardless of when or how their ancestors came, these people were part of the two greatest generations—generations that lived through the World Wars and the Great Depression and pandemics. Fresh from these hardships, they possessed the spirit of capitalism coupled with an ingrained belief in life, liberty, and the pursuit of happiness, and great pride in America. To many, whether from early American stock, slaves, or second- or first-generation immigrants, this meant nothing more and nothing less than to be left to honestly pursue their dreams through individual responsibility and hard work. They were the traits of the first settlers in Cortlandt and the immigrants and ancestors of slaves that followed, and it still held true to some degree by the late 1960s and early 1970s, despite the cultural evolution of the times. The culture of the 1960s and early 1970s was beginning to change the values of the country in subtle ways, and the economic advances of the country since the end of the war contributed to more free time to engage in more frivolous enterprises. Living was no longer the mere act of day-to-day survival as it had been in past generations, with people's sole purpose geared toward survival. Although they were both born in the middle of the 1950s, Nick and Scott were coming of age in the late 1960s and early 1970s. In many respects, this was a crazy time. There was economic inflation, the Vietnam War, anti-war sit-ins and race riots, women's rights, bra-burning, drugs, and free love. It was written somewhere that this was a time of wild parties, hyper-self-expression, and experimentation. Although the boys were somewhat sheltered in their idyllic Cortlandt, these cultural changes were filtering in.

The name Cortlandt is derived from the Dutch Van Cortlandt family, who began purchasing the land in 1677. Their land purchase included property from the Croton River north to Anthony's Nose on the Hudson River and east to Connecticut. This area played a major role during the Revolutionary War, and the historical names of Major John Andre, Benedict Arnold, and George Washington are all associated with Cortlandt. Local Roads, such as Watch Hill, Gallows Hill, and Furnace Dock Road, reflect the Revolutionary War history.

One Town, in particular, the Town of Croton located in the southwest portion of Cortlandt, played a major role in the early settlement and the Revolutionary War. It also played a major role in the future of New York City. The Croton River and its feeder streams were responsible for turning NYC into the major metropolis it became.

Today, the banks of the Croton River are lined with lush marshes, overhanging shrubbery, and looming trees with vast areas of Phragmites bordering the south side, particularly near where the Croton meets the magnificent Hudson River. In the early 1800s, the Croton River was the scene of early American enterprise with mills and farms and brick factories that would feed the growing needs of NYC to the south and Albany to the north. Stagecoaches and sloops were the main forms of transportation between New York City and Albany in the early days of the country. By 1840, there were over one hundred steamboats, and that same decade the Hudson River Railroad opened, ending the use of stagecoaches, sloops, and eventually steamboats.

The boys grew up north of Croton, just outside the City of Peekskill. Oregon Road was one main road that leads from the nearby City of Peekskill to the surrounding Town of Cortlandt and other towns. Oregon Road was the focal point of Nick's and Scott's lives. Most of their early lives were spent just off this road, whether it was learning at their elementary schools, or swimming at Lakeland Acres, or trout-fishing in the Hollow Brook, or going to the drive-in movies, or getting ice cream at the nearby Carvel Stand, or building forts just off the aqueduct. Although they spent much time around the aqueduct, they had no knowledge of its real use or history, and they certainly had no knowledge of its meaning in both their families' history. The aqueduct transferred water from the Catskill Mountains to Yonkers, where it connects to other parts of the system that supplies New York City. This was the evolution of the earlier Croton River system that brought water to New York City, and it was this earlier Croton system that shaped both their families' history and enabled NYC to become what it is today. They also paid little attention to the historic Revolutionary War graveyard that dominated the area between their neighborhoods.

Nick and Scott were both athletes but played different sports in the large Lakeland School District. As the freer time in this era allowed, the boys' focus, when they were not in school or working, was sports. Their industrious nature honed their appetite for sports. Because of its size, competition both athletically and scholastically was intense. This was the midpoint of the baby boom generation, and slots on teams in this large school required fierce competition. Scott was a soccer star. He was the left forward on a very good high school soccer team. During his high school career, he scored well over fifty goals and averaged about sixteen goals a season. His senior year, the team went all the way to the state quarterfinals, where they lost to Portchester. Scott was selected for the all-league team and was honorable mention for the all-county team.

Although they played soccer together as a freshman, Nick moved on to his first love, football, after his freshman year, and was also on the wrestling and baseball teams. By their junior year, they both decided it would be fun to play on the golf team together. During his senior year, Nick finished first in his high school in the Presidential/Marine Corp Physical Fitness test, which was a new test that the coaches were giving for the first time in gym class. Today, Marines take a physical test that includes three exercises: pull-ups, crunches, and a 3.0-mile run designed to test strength, stamina, and battle-readiness. The test that

Nick took in 1973 included five exercises: push-ups, sit-ups, pull-ups, standing broad jump, and a 500-yard run. Based on their results in gym class, the coaches decided to send Nick and four other kids to the New York/ New Jersey Metropolitan Physical fitness competition at Hofstra University in Hempstead on Long Island. Nick finished ninth out of 250 participants. Soon after, the athletic director at Nick's school nominated Nick to received one of three awards presented by the Peekskill Rotary Club honoring the top area student-athletes. The award was covered in the Friday, June 1, 1973, Peekskill Evening Star. The article was titled "Rotary Fete School Athletes: Bristol, Wessells and McCarthy."

This time was a special time in America. The Vietnam War was winding down, and the boys' lives were defined by the conservativism of the 1950s and the counterculture of the 1960s. The 1960s have been described by others as "one of the most tumultuous and divisive decades in world history, marked by the civil rights movement, the Vietnam War and antiwar protests, political assassinations and the emerging 'generation gap' (History Channel). The 1960s brought on a revolution in social norms about clothing, music, drugs, dress, sexuality, formalities, and schooling. This era was a definite ending of American culture and perhaps the full-fledged re-start of progressive liberalism that had tried to influence America in past decades. One thing was evident in this time: unlike the preceding generations, the baby boomers did not have to spend most of their time on the intense need to ensure their survival. Leisure time was much more prevalent, and the culture was changing. Nick's and Scott's parents worked hard to keep their sons grounded in the work ethic of their ancestors, but the culture was changing.

In many ways, Scott and Nick were your typical jocks (high school athletes) of that time—but in some ways they were not. They were also best friends who loved life and loved people. They had the ability to make others feel good around them. Although the times molded their personalities, they were unique in this era. To be sure, there were others who had similar qualities, and Nick and Scott developed lifelong friendships with others in their special/ sphere. They had not fully embraced the irresponsible excess, flamboyance, and disdain for social norms of the 1960s, but the times had some influence on their personalities and their habits.

Despite these cultural influences, Nick's and Scott's family values and genetic inheritance shown through in the era of cultural flux. Despite the cultural influences, they were unique guys in a unique place, in the truly idyllic Town of Cortlandt. Although both Nick and Scott were hard workers, they certainly had more free time than their ancestors, and the social norms were much different. They certainly did not live through the hardships and tough times of their parents and grandparents nor of the generations that came before them. They were hugely lucky because their age allowed them to just avoid the Vietnam War, and neither of their families was directly touched by the war that affected many they knew.

Both Scott and Nick had steady girlfriends, Tracy and Eve, who were two years younger. Both girls were beautiful, honest, and special. The couples went to four sets of junior and senior proms together. They were young kids in love, and Nick and Scott very much respected these girls. But of course, that was part of their personalities. They were raised to be polite and respectful, but they also had enough of the sixties to be sinful. They honored their girlfriends—those were the kinds of guys they were: raised to respect, love, and defend women and intelligent enough to be more mature than most guys their age. As alluded to earlier, neither of these guys liked to fight, but there were more than a few times when they needed to physically defend their turf as the rough and unsettled times of the late 1960s, and early 1970s invaded Cortlandt. During the end of their high school years, the boys worked together at a pizzeria and hung out with their girls and other friends. It was a special time in a special place as the dark feel of the Vietnam War and the distress it brought to families was waning as the war was ending.

CHAPTER 3
The Industrious Bailey's

"Jedidiah!" a colleague of mine yelled to me as she walked into the office from the morning rain. I had been intensely focused on my work. "How is your last case coming?" she asked more softly as she walked past my side. "This is turning out to be an unbelievable case," I said, following with, "What a perfect way to end my career." I looked up momentarily from the papers spread across my desk and the computer screen on my phone into her beautiful, warm, brown eyes and healthy smile. As she walked by—evidently realizing I was not interested in small talk—I returned to the case with resolved focus. The history of the boys and a full evolution of the process naturally required that my research go back into the 19th century. As a master historian, it was not difficult for me to come to the conclusion that the lives of their ancestors in that key time period were a fundamental part of the story. Although the facts spit out by the process naturally led me to this transformative historical era, there was something about the intensity hidden at first in all the dry data that gave me the feeling of connectivity. I was deep into the history now and knew it would be necessary to wade through the immense amount of background data to set the stage for the process to have its full effect. I set myself willingly to the task. After all, history was my life.

Nick McCarthy's grandfather on his mother's side, George Eldridge Bailey, was born in 1892 in Mount Vernon, New York. He served in the trenches in Europe in World War I and lived through the Great Depression and the Spanish Flu pandemic. He was one of eight children of Howard Bailey and Alida Carpenter, and four of his siblings died in childhood. George Bailey was a direct descendant of Abraham Bailey. He, with his father James and two brothers, had migrated from England in the 1830s to start a wire mill on the Croton River and worked nonstop building a business and tending their farms.

George Bailey had reddish-brown hair and carried the Bailey dimple in his chin, the cultural marker of the Norse and of the Vikings and the Celtic druids.

Nick's grandfather George was in the construction business; he was a very smart, no-nonsense guy who did not suffer fools lightly. Nick's mom often told Nick and his brothers that their grandfather built his first house when he was sixteen. There were stories in the family that Grandpa was a tough construction boss who always carried a gun and survived the rough and tumble construction business in New York, including a few run-ins with Mafia union people. Nick's grandfather, George Bailey, and his older brother Ralph married the Quinn sisters: Alice and Margaret (Peg). Alice Louise Quinn was born on December 25, 1890, in Yonkers, New York. She was the third oldest of 10 children born to Ellen and James Quinn of 114 High Street, Yonkers, New York. They had big families in those days. The ceremony took place in St. Joseph's Church and was performed by the Rev. James Mulhern. It was the first marriage ceremony performed at the new altar in the church. Alice's sister Margret Quinn was maid of honor, and George's brother Ralph Bailey was the best man.

George Bailey had a degree from Lehigh University's School of Engineering. There is some mystery about how he got this degree, considering he came from a humble family, but there was no doubt of his intelligence. Other stories suggest he had built a strong relationship with the dean of engineering at Lehigh when he was involved with construction projects on the campus and had numerous discussions about construction and engineering from a variety of vantage points—philosophy, practicality, etc. The dean was rumored to be so impressed with Nick's grandfather that he claimed that George knew more about engineering than he did.

When the depression hit, the federal government put out a notice for a job opening to be the top federal engineer responsible for housing construction projects. Applicants had to take a test, and the top score would get the job. George Bailey took the test, scored the highest, and got the job with a powerful letter of reference from the Lehigh School of Engineering dean. During this time and with that job secured, Alice and George moved back to Yonkers, New York, and bought a gas station. Alice managed and operated the gas station while George traveled to the federal housing construction jobs building low-rent housing across New York State. He was involved with the construction of some of the largest housing projects in Buffalo in the 1930s and in New York City through the 1950s. He was legendary in the business for getting tough jobs done correctly, on time, and under budget. The buildings he built are just now being replaced in Buffalo and New York. A headline in the April 2, 1952, Yonkers Herold Statesmen News Paper read as follows: "Housing Engineer at Schlobohm Job Has Wide Training." The associated article read, "George E. Bailey, Park Avenue, who has been assigned as a project engineer at the Schlobohm Housing Project, will be in charge of all Federal Housing Authority matters in connection with the new project. He is also a project engineer on the largest of P.H.A. housing project – Edenwald in the Bronx - which consists of 2,039 family units in 42 buildings on a property covering an area of 35 acres. This project was started in December 1950, with initial occupancy scheduled for August of this year and final completion in September 1953. Among the many large construction jobs he was connected with was a New York City Housing development consisting of 15 separate construction projects being built simultaneously". After working for the federal government, he built other buildings, including the courthouses in lower Manhattan. For some of this time, in the early days, Alice raised the three kids, ran the gas station, and held down the household. These were hard workers in hard times; they were smart, energetic, and entrepreneurial; products of the times and their ancestors.

James Bailey Sr., the progenitor of the George Bailey family in America, came over from England to America in 1830 with three of his sons and carved out the future of this group of Bailey's in an area of Yorktown called Huntersville, where the Croton River met Hunter's Brook. James Bailey Sr. was born in 1771 in West Yorkshire, England. James had distant relatives who originally settled in the part of Van Cortland Manor that ultimately became Somers and Yorktown and was called the Middle District, or Hanover. Word had filtered back to England about the Croton River Valley.

The Croton River Valley had been originally settled by English, Dutch, French Huguenots, and Quakers. One such settler was Hachaliah Bailey, a farmer and cattle merchant who became famous for buying an elephant in the N.Y.C. stockyards; he named the elephant Old Bet. Hachaliah's father was born in Croton Falls in 1747. The Hachaliah Bailey side of the Bailey family traces back to Nicholas "Judge" Bailey, who was born in England in 1628 and died in Westchester, New York, in 1689. There were other Bailey's prominent in the Croton-Yorktown area who pre-dated James Bailey Sr. There was a Levi Bailey, who in 1775 commanded the delegates of the North Battalion of Westchester

County. There was a different James and his brother Gilbert Bailey who were wardens of the Saint James Episcopal Reform Church in 1792, whose members included Joshua Purdy of the long-time area Purdy family. By the late 1820s, two other Bailey relatives, Horace and Solomon, were part of the Farmers and Drovers Bank of Somers.

But Hachaliah Bailey was one of the more famous of that clan. Hachaliah's father purchased land just outside the small Village of Somers in 1773, and Hachaliah was born in 1775. As a man, Hachaliah Lyman Bailey was a bit of a wild-looking fellow: a strong, lean man with long brown shoulder-length hair that he wore combed back. He had small piercing eyes and a big bushy reddish-brown beard. He was also a very industrious fellow, as were his kin. In addition to farming, he raised cattle and was prominent in the Farmers and Drovers Society. Hachaliah was associated with the creation of a toll road through Somers and was one of the directors of the Croton Turnpike Company. Stagecoaches ran passengers north and south between Danbury and Peekskill and south along the Turnpike and then on the Albany, Danbury, and Boston post roads. Horse- and ox-drawn wagons and carts also traveled the Turnpike to take the milk and other products to Croton Point and Sing Sing for river shipping to New York City. Cattle were driven along the Turnpike as the major route from Somers and the surrounding area. This was the main route for drovers getting the cattle to New York City either via the docks in Croton and Sing Sing or on direct cattle drives to the stockyards in N.Y.C. Sing Sing on the Hudson and Sawpit (now Port Chester) on the Long Island Sound were the two main routes for farmers to get their crops to New York.   Hachaliah was also part-owner of a sloop that was used to transport cattle up and down the Hudson. This industrious Bailey had his hand in many things. The New York City stockyards were located in the Bowery section of New York City and were the destination for all of the livestock driven along the Turnpike. By the mid-1700s, New York City needed a larger food supply as the population grew, and the lower Bowery became the location of the meat industry. In 1750, a public slaughterhouse was established on the banks of the Collect Pond, and the Bull's Head Tavern opened as a drover's tavern, with a large stockyard next door at 46-48 Bowery, where cattlemen could bring their animals to be sold. Once at the stockyards, the drovers would gather at the nearby Bull's Head Tavern. Hachaliah was rumored to complete a lot of his business at the tavern, which consisted of a hotel and saloon. It was here where he was rumored to have purchased Old Bet for 1,000 dollars. With Old Bet, he started one of the first circuses in America, when he formed the Bailey

Circus with Old Bet as the main attraction, a trained dog, pigs, horses, and wagons. It is also rumored that the Bailey Circus was a role model for P.T. Barnum and his eventual Ringling's Brother and Barnum & Bailey Circus, which Barnum formed with a different Bailey. Hachalaih also built the Elephant Hotel completed in 1825 in Somers, New York, and served two terms in State Legislature. He eventually moved to Northern Virginia and bought the land outside Falls Church at the intersection of Leesburg Pike and Columbia Pike in Fairfax County, Virginia. That land is now known as Bailey's Crossroads. He returned to Somers in 1845 for a visit. During that visit, he died from the kick of a horse at age 70. He is buried in the Somers Ivandell Cemetery.

By the early 1800s, the water in New York City was becoming stagnated and filthy. Numerous disease outbreaks and major fires defined the need for a new water source for the City. The waters of the Croton River were selected. By the end of 1836, immigrants, mostly Irish, started to arrive in the area to work on the Croton dam and aqueduct to supply water to New York City. Little did the residents of the Croton area know that the severe need of clean water in New York City would change their lives and alter their families' futures. Hachalaih Bailey and the other Bailey's had a prominent effect on the early days of Westchester County, Cortlandt, and the Croton River Valley. But possibly none more than James Bailey Sr., and certainly none were as adversely affected by New York City politicians or the thirst for power, influence, and water.

James Bailey Sr. was the great-great-grandfather of George Eldridge Bailey. He was a serious man, solid in stature and of medium height. He was a roughly handsome man, and he carried the family trait of a dimple in his chin and reddish-brown hair, which was a cultural marker of the Norse and of the Vikings. He worked hard and did not suffer fools lightly. Highly intelligent and generally likable, he made friends sparingly but was immensely loyal to those he befriended. Above all, he was industrious. Most of his time was focused on his family and work. It was in his genes, part of his nature, and heightened by his faith. He was an ardent follower of the Protestant work doctrine that diligence in one's work was a sign of being one of God's chosen. Work was a natural part of his life, something he enjoyed. He settled in the Croton River Valley because of what it offered. What he did not know was that by the early 1800s, a growing and desperate New York City began to look to "upstate" rivers for water supplies. The Croton River, a tributary of the Hudson River, would eventually be chosen as the answer to N.Y.C.'s water shortage.

By the 1800s, Yorkshire, England, was in a time of rapid urbanization and industrialization. Throughout history, this part of England had suffered numerous occupations by conquering armies, and the nature and heritage of the men and women were a direct result. Yorkshire was occupied by the Romans, followed by Germanic peoples. Later the Vikings and Norsemen came from Sweden, Denmark, and Norway to occupy Yorkshire. What resulted was a complex mixture of language and culture that wound its way in the genes of the people who lived there.

The name Bailey probably came to England from Normandy, France, after the Norman conquest in 1066, and the name was believed to be first found in Northumberland. Northumberland is in northeast England, which includes North Yorkshire and is the frontier zone between England and Scotland. This area was shaped by a history of violence and conflict. In ancient times the area was reportedly occupied by the Brythonic- Celtic Votadini and the upland people or hill dwellers known as the Brigantes. In Pre- Roman times, the Brigantes controlled the largest section of northern England in an area centered in what is now Yorkshire. These Celtic or Ancient Britons were indigenous Celtic people living in the undeveloped landscape of the high moorland. This area was witness to the Roman invasion and plundering Viking attacks. Later the Anglo Saxon- Scottish border wars were fought to the death and included raids by the notorious Border Reivers who were responsible for cattle rustling, feuding, murder, arson, and pillaging. The people of this area were notorious for their ability to endure cold, hunger, and hardship. Border Reivers and their families were fierce. Their allegiance was to their family, and they typically claimed either nationality or no nationality, depending on the perceived advantage. They had relatives on both sides of the Scottish-English border. Basic human survival meant they were kindred to a family seeking security through group strength and cunning. They were not dependent on a distant monarch- rugged individuals was an understatement. Perhaps this explains the reported motto of the Bailey's of that time; "One's country is where one is well".

James worked as a wire drawer in Sheffield, a metropolitan borough in South Yorkshire, for the firm owned by the Butcher family. Wire drawing is making metal wire by drawing it through dies. By pulling the wire through a single or series of drawing dies, substantially enhances the strength. In the first half of the 19th century, Britain led the world's industrial revolution, mostly due to the production of products made from iron and steel. Britain also had people with capital and an energetic population of entrepreneurs. By the mid-1800s, Britain accounted for 47% of world production of pig iron and almost 40% of steel.

James started his career as an apprenticeship indenture at an iron mill for seven years, starting at the age of 16. It was the first step for poor English kids on their road to economic independence. He worked for a master craftsman, and after the seven years of apprenticeship was completed, he traveled from employer to employer, earning wages as a journeyman. The last few years he spent with the Butcher family. Parts of the Bailey family had immigrated to America starting as early as the 1600s, and James heard about the place they settled—the Croton River Valley—through cousins still in England.

The Butcher firm was known for the production of steel products and cutlery, mostly for the American market. A large part of Sheffield's steel output was sent across the Atlantic, and Butcher made a fortune from the American trade. James was a clever, hardworking mechanic with a handicraft skills. At this time in Sheffield, the steel industry was still dependent on the handicraft skills of individuals. A clever, hardworking, risk-taking mechanic had a solid opportunity. But James's dream was to go to America to seek fortune because he saw the huge profits made by Butcher in the American market. He knew he could take his skill and sell the fruits of his labor directly in the American market. He had a strong desire to be his own man—it drove him and his future. He was a self-confident man dying a slow death working for others in the industrial bowels of England. The American market was largely responsible for the remarkable expansion of the Sheffield crucible steel industry. James saw his chance. As Sheffield grew populous, the narrow streets became more crowded and the houses dark and black. James longed to get his family out, but he knew he was no longer a young man—but his sons were. He thought of the stories he heard about the Croton River, and he knew much of Butcher's products were shipped to America and to New York City. He set out to contact his family relatives in the Croton River Valley as a means of entry into the land. He heard back from his distant relatives that the Croton River was the place for his enterprise and that land was available.

The Napoleonic Wars that ended around 1815 had caused much distress in England. The price of food had risen, and wages had fallen while at the same time, the population was increasing at a rapid rate. This put great stress on

James Sr. and his young family. He had already lost a wife and two children to the disease-infested and polluted City. Sheffield had suffered badly during the Napoleonic Wars because many of the European countries had stopped buying its goods, and terrible poverty existed. It was during this time that James Sr.'s plans for America began. When the war ended, the European trade started again; Sheffield grew rapidly. By the late 1820s, close to 100,000 people lived within the city boundaries. For thousands, there were no toilets and no clean water, and the rubbish and excrement from the overcrowding was dumped into the streets and flowed like an open sewer. At that time, there was a high infant mortality rate, and the average life expectancy was 27.

Besides the cutlery business, Butcher's firm also produced products such as structural steel used in beams, angle stock, channel stock, bar stock, rails, and so on. As with most steel mills in England at that time, Butcher had a rolling mill division that converted semi-finished casting products into finished products. This was the division where Bailey worked. Much like the process of wire making, rolling is a metal forming process in which metal stock is passed through one or more pairs of rolls to reduce the thickness and to make the thickness uniform. The metal is rolled into sheets and bars.

Sheffield was part of the West Riding of Yorkshire and is named from the River Sheaf, which runs through the City. Sheffield was perfectly located for water-powered industries because it was situated among fast-flowing rivers and streams and was surrounded by hills containing raw materials such as coal, iron ore, and other necessary materials. As the steel industry grew, Sheffield became more dark, dank, and polluted. Steel production involved long working hours in unpleasant conditions that offered little or no safety protection. James plotted to leave; he wanted to find success in a fresh, clean America. He wanted individual freedom and the power to be free to run his own business; he wanted this for his sons, who were just starting to learn the trade.

James first married Patience Aspinall in 1796, and they had two daughters: Mary and Hannah. James's wife Patience died in 1800, and a year later, on July 20, 1801, James married Susannah Clay of the Village of Greetland. Susannah was from the Lindwell section of Greetland, and they were married at St. Mary the Virgin Church at Elland. Susie, as she was called, was part of the Clay family and an ancestor of John Clay, who built "Clay House" around 1650. The Clay family of England included knights during the reign of King Edward the IV and coal barons during the reign of Queen Elizabeth.

Abraham (Abram) was born on April 12, 1807, and was the fourth of nine children of James Sr. and Susannah. The other children were George, John, Jane, Grace, James Jr., Ellen, Joseph, and Grace Elizabeth. George died soon after birth, and Grace Elizabeth died at age nine, both succumbing to the many illnesses that led to the high mortality rate. James and Susie and their nine children—seven children together plus two from his first marriage—lived in "The Gate" in Greetland before moving for James's most recent job with Butcher. While James was plotting his move to America and gaining knowledge, his family was growing and growing. The ancestral heritage of James and Susannah, which was shared by their children, was fortified by their sedulous culture. It formed their souls and their minds and marked their futures. This nature demanded the respect that people gave them.

The needs of a young family and a good job kept James Sr. anchored to England. As the children grew, James Sr. became more restless. His drive and desire pained him, and the death of two of his children consumed him. His wife Susannah, however, wanted no part of leaving England. The overwhelmingly progressive impoverishment and dispossession of the English workforce leading up to 1830, coupled with the ever-increasing dark and dankness of polluted Sheffield, weighed heavily on James. This was topped off by the allure of America. With his age advancing, he saw his dreams fading. He had made up his mind. He was leaving with his oldest sons with the hope that his wife and the rest of his children would follow.

Around 1830 before the onset of the agricultural Swing Riots in southern England, James Bailey Sr., then fifty-nine, and three of his sons, John, Abram, and James Jr., left England for America. The rest of the family, including his daughter by his first marriage, Mary, and her husband, George Twigger, migrated in the ensuing years. Eventually, the entire family came to America except for Susannah. Even Jane, who had initially stayed behind with Susannah, came to America with her husband, Matthew Mitchell, after Susannah's death.

CHAPTER 4
The Iron Men of Croton

As word of the American Bailey's filtered back over the years to the Bailey clan still in Yorkshire, England, James Sr. dreamed of freedom in the wild and scarcely settled areas north of New York City in America. James Bailey Sr.'s life and family had prevented him from coming earlier. When he and his sons came over in 1830, they settled in an area of Yorktown called Huntersville, where the Croton River met Hunter's Brook. James Bailey Sr. knew it was the perfect place for him and his family.

When Abram and his two brothers immigrated to America with their dad, Abram was twenty-three. His older brother John was twenty-seven, and James Jr. was eighteen. James Sr. had contacted his relatives in the Croton and Somers, New York, area and set in motion obtaining land along the Croton River in Yorktown for farms and his wire mill. The Bailey's quickly settled in the Yorktown/New Castle area immediately adjacent to the Village of Croton along the southern side of the Croton River.

In 1830, the Croton River Valley was a wild and rugged region of wooded granite and limestone ridges and outcrops as well as numerous lakes and streams. Like Sheffield, England, Croton was perfectly located for water-powered industries because it was situated along the fast-flowing Croton River with feeder streams and surrounded by hills and nearby towns containing the necessary raw materials. But unlike Sheffield, Croton was a raw wilderness of clean, fresh water and air. If not for the Bailey's' industrious nature, the contrast would have been overwhelming. They became aware that iron foundries were located in Port Chester, Peekskill, and Morrisania; brickyards in Croton; marble quarries in Tuckahoe, Sing Sing, Hastings, and Thornwood. There was also a rock quarry in nearby Verplank. Their wire and rolling iron mill would fit in perfectly. They immediately set about their work, and their ethic drove them forward.

Even though it played a huge role in the Revolutionary war, by 1830, the Village of Croton still consisted of only a dozen houses, two stores, a tavern, and a boat landing. The streets were dirt. Most of the small population along the Croton River were farmers, and a few also owned mills, mostly for grain and lumber. The farmers scratched out an existence in the rugged environment. Croton Landing on the Hudson River provided the farmers and merchants access to the boats that transported their produce, animals, and merchandise to the rapidly burgeoning city of New York to the south and toward the Hudson Highlands, Verplanck, Peekskill (Peeks Kill), and all the way to Albany to the north. The nearby village of Sing Sing was the largest population in the area, with over 4,000 residents. In 1825, the State of New York chose Sing Sing for the location of its third State Prison. The Sing Sing prison was constructed directly in the middle of an existing large marble quarry. It was nicknamed "The Big House" and "Castle on the Hudson," and the phrase "getting sent up the river" became popular as criminals in New York City were sent to Sing Sing—up the Hudson.

It was with the help of Hachaliah and other old family relatives that James Bailey's family made their way to the Croton River Valley. Around 1831, the Bailey's finalized their acquisition of the right location on the Croton River and started the mill after buying supplies and erecting buildings as well as stockpiling the raw materials. In addition, they built and worked small farms that would sustain their needs.

The Bailey wire and rolling mill were located near the rapids and old High Bridge on the Croton River. James Bailey Sr. brought his knowledge of wire drawing and metal rolling to the mill in America. All the items necessary to produce iron—limestone, timber, coal, and iron ore—were readily available in the local area. Iron was mined extensively from the second half of the eighteenth century. The West Point and Outcrop Hamilton Mines (off Sunken Mine Road in Fahnestock State Park) supplied the high-grade iron ore to the West Point Foundry in Cold Spring; the Denny Iron Mine (on the east side of Dennytown Road near Sunken Mine Road), and the Croft Iron Mine (on the west side of what is now Sprout Brook Road just above the Philipstown line) supplied iron for various ironworks.

The Bailey's found this beautiful place was remarkable for its abundance of deer, beaver, wild turkeys, geese, swans, ducks, and other game, and the Croton and Hudson Rivers had plenty of salmon, shad, herring, and striped bass. The stark beauty of the place was a wonderment to the newly arrived Bailey's with numerous surrounding freshwater streams and lakes that teamed with trout, black bass, and pickerel. There were broad meadows and cold, rocky, lofty hills, steep slopes, and dark, magnificent woods. Large boulders of cold black or steely gray granite were strewn about randomly and near outcrops. Although the terrain was slightly similar to that of their previous Greetland home, with much of that English village on one side of the steep hill, this place was so much better and worse. They would have to get used to the sparse population and rugged, wild environment. They devoted their time and energy to their work, which helped them cope with the drastic change. And they also had church.

Still strong but advancing in age, James Sr. relied on his sons for their youthful strength and work ethic as he taught them the trade. When they arrived, they settled into the community. James's oldest son, John, already had some experience in the iron industry in England, as did Abram. The Bailey's spoke English with the distinct regional dialect and accent of Yorkshire, England. This was the English dialect of northern England, which has roots in older languages such as Old English and Old Norse. The Bailey's particular English dialect was influenced heavily by the Old Norse ancestor of their region in England. When they arrived, their accents made them unique and distinct from the earlier English settlers, such as the Tompkins family. The Tompkins family roots went back to well before the Revolutionary War times. It was into this region of early American settlers and that of the ancestors of the early Dutch and French Huguenot that the Bailey's began their future. Although their accents branded them as new arrivals, their distant Bailey relatives from generations ago had been in America since the 1620s and had long ago been natives. Through the help of their relatives and their shared common religion, they were quickly accepted by the locals. Most of the local inhabitants were either Quakers, Episcopal or Methodists, English, and Dutch Presbyterian, or French Protestants. Despite their accent, they rapidly became well-liked among their neighbors, who associated them with common sense, loyalty, and the reliability of a hardworking church family.

Abram looked over at his two brothers, John and James Jr., as they stood at the side of the family farm in the very early morning well before sunrise. Once the mill and farm buildings were basically complete with the generous help of some of their Bailey relatives and locals, it was time to start to stockpile whatever food they could for the bulk of the winter months ahead. They had been out hunting and fishing a few times, but it was here and there when they could steal a little time. They were still new arrivals in this wild place, and so during the early hunts, they went with some of the locals, mainly from the Tompkins and Purdy families. This was different; this was a planned hunt where their mission was to hopefully bring as much deer meat and other game to last the winter. The three Bailey brothers were heading off to prime hunting areas with some advice of where to go from their new neighbors. If they were lucky, they might get a black bear, which was not as prevalent in the area as in the early days. The black bear had been overhunted because of the big demand for their thick hides, rich meat, and fat. Because of their low reproductive rate and overhunting, their populations were depleted by the time the Bailey's arrived.

The Bailey brothers were headed up into the hills on the south side of the river behind their mill and farms far enough beyond the local settlers to be deep in the woods. It had just snowed about two inches the day before. This being the best conditions to find and track recent movement; enough snow that the animals left fresh tracks, but not deep enough to make walking difficult, the Bailey's took time from the mill. All three had flintlock, Lancaster-style long rifles called the "Kentucky Rifle." They had hunted some in England with their dad growing up, but they were unaccustomed to these American-made rifles with their unusually long barrels.

They were headed up the slope toward the higher meadows, where they were told the deer would be. As they walked, there was little conversation, which was as much a consequence of the exertion of climbing up the steep slope as it was that the Bailey brothers were men of few words when they were together. They knew each other well and had worked together long enough to communicate without much verbalization. When they first started off, they entered the thick forest and climbed a steep slope. There was no thought of trying to bring horses because of the slope but also because of the numerous holes, stumps, and fallen logs that were all about. As Abram looked around, he noticed plenty of rotting wood and decaying leaf litter with various mushrooms and other fungi. The forest was thick, and not much of the snow had made the ground.

Because of the conditions, they stayed to the established trail originally carved by animals and Indians years before and after by the locals to get to the high meadows. The trail naturally switched back, so their climb was not direct. At first, while it was still dark, visibility was poor and travel slow. In the summer, they probably would not have been able to see more than 20 or 30 yards in any direction. But since it was late fall just before the start of winter and some of the leaves were already gone from the trees, they could see about 100 yards as the bright full moon intermingled with the early morning light off the dusting of snow on the forest floor. It was eerie how the conditions made the scene so visibly clear in the frosty silence of the late fall dawn.

As they walked through the woods, Abram thought how beautiful these woods were despite the drab, muted stark colors of early winter. Although the dull shades of brown and grey were in stark contrast to the lush, vibrant green of the summer, the sprinkling of snow and the moon-lite morning brought a different type of beauty. He took a deep breath when they all stopped to catch their breaths. He focused on the scene around him as he looked past the water vapor in his brother's exhaled breath as it came in contact with air and formed tiny water and ice droplets. To Abram, the forest had a pleasant smell that frequently accompanies the first snow as it melts. It smelled like a combination of fresh wet dirt and slightly damp-dry twigs, and Abram thought how it contrasted with the smell in the foul dank Sheffield. This part of the forest was mostly dominated by a variety of broadleaf trees with a few patches of evergreen trees. As Abram glanced up toward the tops of the trees and downward, the different layers of plants came into focus. The top canopy was formed by the tall trees at least 20 or 30 feet overhead, maybe higher. As his glance moved downward, he saw the second canopy formed by the saplings and smaller trees and then still lower at the understory of shrubs and honeysuckle bushes. When his glance reached the ground, he focused on the ground cover of mosses, ferns, and lichens at his feet, as well as small flowering forest herbs, grasses, shrubs, and other plants as he glanced farther up the slope. These would soon be covered with the full weight of falling leaves above. As they resumed their walk, he stared to notice the wildflowers and herbs, and he knew they were getting close to the meadow as the canopy was thinning out. Most of the trees here were ash, allowing enough light for these types of plants. The previous section of the forest had more oak and beech trees, which had a thicker canopy of leaves, causing the forest floor to be mostly bare and, in some spots, covered in ferns that required less light than in this section of the forest. Because it was the first spot of cold weather and just a little snowy, many of these plants were still visible. Although the annual plants had died a short time ago with the first frosts and scattered their seeds, these perennial plants were still in the process of going dormant.

Abram could hear the woodpeckers, crows, and blue jays with their distinctive sounds as well as other birds as they began to sound in the early morning's first light. A few weeks before, he would have also heard the crickets and tree frogs because the weather was still warm. He could also hear the squeaky-squeaky creaking noise of branches as the wind caused them to rub together.

The hike took them a good hour, and they reached their destination as the light of day was just beginning to find its way to the large, broad meadow. They stood on the edge of the meadow, still in the darkness of the woods, and walked along the edge looking for tracks or animals. In the summer, the meadow would be filled with wildflowers, grasses, and an occasional shrub and bathed in warm, hot sunshine. But today, the sky had the steely look of autumn as the winter approached. Soon they came upon an area of tall grass near the edge of the forest. There was dense brush and foliage along two sides. It was a perfect place for resting deer to hunker down because it included nice grass for bedding and the dense brush to help partially hide the deer from their predators' gazes. The brothers noticed the distinct physical impression in the grass and some fresh deer tracks leading west across the meadow. Once they caught their breaths from the hike, John started, "Abram, you are the best shot, so you should position yourself in the prime shooting location." They planned to circle the meadow inside the tree line until they could see the deer. "James and I," John continued, "will head around to the other side of the deer. James, since you are a better shot than me, you set up halfway, and I will get behind them and make enough noise to flush them toward you guys." Both Abram and James had two rifles apiece. Because they knew they would not have time to reload, they preloaded both when they reached their hunting spot while John was maneuvering across to the far side.

The plan worked beautifully; they had wandered across a big heard. Between James and Abram, they shot one deer apiece, and even John was able to shoot one as the deer herd started back toward him once the firing started. This would be a great help to their food needs their first winter considering they still did not know what hardships to expect.

The Croton Wire Mills or Croton Wire Works, as it was known, grew rapidly.

They sold their products to the growing population along the Hudson from Albany to New York City and into New Jersey through agents. Their main New York City agent was JNO. F. Mackie & Co. is located at 69 Broad Street in New York City, just east of where the East River meets the Hudson River in lower Manhattan. Ironically, later generations of industrious Bailey's would ply their trade in buildings further up Broad Street at Wall Street. Typically, various ads were run in newspapers by their agents. One such Mackie advertisement appeared in the New York Evening Post and read as follows:

"Croton Wire Mills – The subscribers constantly have on hand and for sale, the usual varieties of wire, manufactured from American charcoal iron at the above works. Their stock comprises a general assortment of the bright and annealed bundle and stone Wire. They are also prepared to receive and execute orders for telegraph and bridge wire of superior quality, samples of which can be seen at the office - JNO. F. Mackie & Co, 69 Broad Street"

Another Mackie advertisement for both the Hudson River Iron Company at Jersey City and the Croton Iron Works listed various iron products, including scroll iron, band iron, iron wire, sieve, and Broom wire, Telegraph and screw wire, best Juniatta billets for wire, and blooms for nails and wire as well as bar iron for shafting"

The Bailey's made a variety of these products using various techniques, and their sprawling mills on the Croton had various rooms for products. In one room, they made billets, which were hot-rolled iron that is taken out directly during the casting process. Billets are highly ductile and soft and produced in a square cross-section of area less than 36 sq. inches (230 sq. cm). They fall under the category of semi-finished casting products. Their other final products included bars, rods, tubes, pipes, wire, and wire products. Steel bars are the "long" product of steel billets. Some billets are folded/rolled to form much stronger reinforcement bars. They are a complete product ready to be used in construction. The bars are produced by the tight rolling of the steel billets.

James Sr. and his children were involved with various experiments in the production of malleable iron. They welcomed an inventor by the name of Rodgers to perform experimental techniques at their mill. These experiments helped change iron manufacturing. One of these processes involved deoxidizing iron ore in a heated hollow screw. At that time, this process greatly improved the quality of iron. When the process was completed, the iron was dropped into the furnace, avoiding all fluxes, and out came "blooms" of the finest iron. Mr. Rodgers, the inventor, claimed that by this process, there would be a savings of from eight to twelve dollars a ton in the production of iron. It was from Bailey's rolling mill, above the rapids in the Croton just above the old High Bridge, where these experiments were conducted.

By the mid-1830s, the Bailey's had joined the prominent families in the Croton area, which included the Underhills, Outhouses, and Tompkins. Other prominent area families included the Lounsbury, Purdy, Ryder, and Rowlee families. Other than the Van Cortlandt's, the most renowned family and one of the largest landowners were the Underhills, who controlled Croton Point. The Purdy family was one of the oldest, as Daniel Purdy had bought a large tract of land from the vast Van Cortlandt Manor in the mid-1700s. Many of these families either worshiped in the Methodist church in the small Chapel in the cemetery or worshiped in the Quaker church. There were also a few black families sprinkled around the Croton Watershed area and along the Hudson. A few worked for the Bailey's. James Sr. and his sons had befriended one particular family that was descended from a black soldier who had fought in the Revolutionary War and was one of the few surviving members of the famous First Rhode Island Regiment, which fought a key battle along the Croton River. Jedidiah had started working for the Bailey's not long after they started the mill, and the boys—particularly Abram—relied on him in the mill as a smart, extremely hard, and reliable worker. He was very strong as well.

In 1778, during the Revolutionary War, several hundred black freemen and slaves from Rhode Island were recruited as regular soldiers in the Continental Army. They formed into the First Rhode Island Regiment and were pledged their freedom at war's end. On April 15, 1781, the brave and stout men of the First Rhode Island were assigned a defensive position at the northern bank of the Croton River on the American lines guarding the northernmost part of Westchester County's Neutral Ground and one strategic structure, the Pines Bridge. It was over Pines Bridge that the spy Maj. John Andre, displaying Benedict Arnold's pass, had crossed the previous fall. The regiment was attacked by the British Col. James De Lancey, who had a sizable force of 60 cavalry and 200 infantrymen. Most of the men of the Rhode Island were killed, wounded, or captured. Those who were captured alive at this battle were sold into slavery in the British West Indies. The dead, both the white officers and black rank and file, were buried together in a place today marked by two separated stone memorials alongside the Crompond Presbyterian Church of

Yorktown, on Route 202 east of the Taconic State Parkway.

Robert Underhill purchased Croton Point in 1804, and with his sons, Richard and William, owned various enterprises in Croton, including Croton Mills Flour, located about a half-mile up the Croton River from the old High Bridge. They were involved with vineyards and the growing of Newtown Pippin apples for foreign export and castor bean plants for castor oil. Their 250 fertile acres yielded crops of watermelons, apples, and grapes for the New York City market. Robert Underhill and his sons' grapes won many awards, and the family was known both for promoting the American grape industry and for developing new varieties of grapes. They had about eighty acres covered with the Isabella and Catawba grapevine. Upon Robert's death, his sons divided the land. Richard acquired an 85-acre tract in the southern portion, and William obtained 165 acres in the north.

William developed his land into a brickyard on the northern end of the point. He and his brother-in-law, Richard Tallcot, used revolutionary steam-powered machinery to make a large number of bricks at two extremely productive brickyards, which each employed several hundred men.

His brother Richard eventually developed a portion of the point property into a very successful vineyard and winery, with underground wine cellars built into the hillside on the property. Richard, who produced a hybrid grape that was resistant to disease, became famous for the cultivation of grapes and the production of wine. The Underhill vineyards attained a worldwide reputation, and Croton Point wines were reportedly featured at the luxurious Astor House Hotel in New York City.

The industrious Bailey's, as they became known in Croton, were a hardworking group. They all possessed a similar personality and drive with minor differences common in all families. The father, James Sr., and his first son John were quiet, no-nonsense individuals—friendly and kind but very focused individuals. They spent most of their time with work, family, and church. Abram, one of the middle sons, was quite the opposite. He was gregarious, sociable, friendly, and outgoing. Like all the Bailey's, he was hardworking but had a way around people. A natural leader, he treated everyone with equal respect and dignity. He could lose his temper when pushed, but few pushed him because he was a strong man. His younger brother James was mild-mannered and quiet, and the youngest, Joseph, was the artist of the family. Wiry, strong, and slight, Joseph was extremely handsome. Although he loved all his older siblings, Joseph particularly looked up to Abram. Joseph did not come over with his father and his three older brothers because he was too young. He stayed in England with his mother and sisters and made his way to Croton later.

The boys all married members from local families or families they met through their church. The church offered a common means to meet people, and the Methodist congregation held a summer retreat in Croton, attracting people from New York City, the other towns in the Hudson Highlands, and as far away as New England and Western New York. John married Clarissa Waring from Stanford, Connecticut. James married Josephine Hunt, and Abram and Joseph married two local sisters of the Tompkins clan, Catherine and Phebe. The Tompkins sisters were the daughters of Robert and Sarah Tompkins and a second cousin to Daniel Tompkins who was the vice president in 1817 under James Monroe. Daniel D. Tompkins was born in 1774 and was the seventh son of the honorable Jonathan G. Tompkins and Sarah Hyatt and grandson of Stephen Tompkins, who traces back to John Tomkins. John Tompkins emigrated from north England and landed at Plymouth before moving to Concord. The Tompkins' forebears comprised one of several founding families in Westchester and eventually Yorktown and Croton. The other long-term families included the Strangs, Travis's, the Lee and Purdy families, Ferris's, and the Hyatt's. Beginning in the 1740s, the Tompkins carved out farms for themselves in an area of Yorktown and New Castle called Huntersville, where the Croton River meets Hunter's Brook.

Here the Bailey's were in the clean, beautiful Croton River Valley and surrounding areas where some of the most important dramas in the history of America were enacted. Washington, Rochambeau, Lafayette, and many other noted personalities, along with many nameless men and women, such as the men of the First Rhode Island Regiment, fought for the freedom in this place. The price of that freedom saturated this land and imparted to its soul. When the Bailey's arrived in 1830 and built their future next to the Tompkins, they had little knowledge of the unique historical past of the area. The place just felt right; it was a perfect reflection of their personalities—hard, complex, pure, and simple, all mixed together with a rugged work ethic.

CHAPTER 5

The Quarry

Jedidiah thought it was time to focus back on Nick and Scott's history as his detailed look at the Bailey's needed to soak in while he reflected on this later generation. While the Bailey history was meticulously researched, the process had laid out a number of what at first appeared to be unrelated events—almost like short stories—about these boys. After spending time on the Bailey's' background, it was time to take that background to reflect on these seemingly disparate episodes of Scott and Nick. He picked them up in the order that the process provided, trusting his long experience and the efficacy of the process. Some of the ties back to the Bailey's were obvious, while others were subtly hidden, as was typical of how the process manufactured its intended result. This became more evident as the process flowed back and forth between the two eras, and Jedidiah allowed himself to let the process tell the story now; he just let it flow along. It started with a story about Nick and Scott's visit to a quarry in Verplanck. Jedidiah recalled a mention of a quarry in Verplanck earlier in the deep history of the Bailey's. He sat back and let the process unfold, adding the historical texture on the way.

Located immediately south of Indian Point Nuclear Power Plant, the old rock quarry was adjacent to the Hudson River in Verplanck. When workers hit an underground aquifer, clear, pristine, very cold, and exquisitely clear turquoise or azure-blue waters flooded the quarry. Nick and Scott often went to the quarry when they were in high school and during their early college years. At the time Nick and Scott went to the quarry, there were rumors that the quarry was used for cooling water for the Nuclear plant. Somehow the boys didn't think that mattered. It was a great place to be on a hot day. The boys were risk-takers, and sometimes their innate need for the quest overrode their normally intelligent minds. They managed to survive some of the not-so-smart choices they sometimes made. Very occasionally, they would go to the quarry off Crompound Road in Mohegan closer to their homes because it was where kids they knew went. On one such trip to the Mohegan Quarry, Nick had carried one of the Snowden girls who cut her foot on glass from the quarry all the way down the dirt path to the road where the cars were parked. The funny thing was Nick did not know this girl because she may have been a grade or two younger, and he never again saw her. Yet she had made an impression during the long walk from the quarry while in his arms making small talk. This was typical Nick.

The boys seldom went to the Mohegan Quarry. The Verplanck Quarry was just so much more of a cool place. A visit to the quarry in the late 1960s and early 1970s always represented a unique experience. You never knew what you would find when you got there. Some days there would be a group of young local hippies swimming naked and getting stoned with the music of The Doors blasting, or one might find a local motorcycle gang hanging out drinking and swimming to Deep Purple or Judas Priest or just some locals hanging out. On other days there would not be a soul around, and it would be peacefully quiet. The boys came there for all those experiences as the waning days of the peace, love, and rock and roll 1960s and the Vietnam War made for interesting times.

There were many reasons the boys were drawn to the quarry and the cliffs. The possible sight of naked girls was certainly one, but the other was the surge-of-testosterone adventure of diving off the rock cliffs or roofs of the partially submerged quarry buildings into the aqua-green crystal-clear water. In 1968, ABCs Wide World of Sports first telecast the International Cliff Diving Championships from Acapulco. This was the boys' version of jumping off the Wide World of Sports cliffs, and it was a rite of passage to take the first jump off the 25–30-foot cliff into the clear water below.

The boys parked the car and entered the quarry area off 14th Street, walking down a path and across the mounds of waste white-colored millings from the former quarry operation. They made their way down to the cliffs overlooking the southeast side of the quarry. As they walked, they talked about what kind of day it would be at the quarry and who would be there. Typically, they avoided the place when the motorcycle gangs were there. The biker guys were worse than mean and always looking to fight. Nick had befriended a boy when he was young in Catholic school who eventually became a gang member. This served Nick well a few times in bars around town when the gang was looking for a fight. The kid remembered Nick and made sure the gang left him alone. But Nick and Scott were smart enough to avoid these guys—they picked fights just to fight.

Nick and Scott were hoping it would be a day when lots of naked girls would be sunning themselves on the rocks or in tire tubes in the water. But today, they saw no signs of bikes and heard no music. As they got to the cliffs, they looked around and saw that the quarry was empty. No one was around, which was just fine with them—no worries about getting into a disagreement with the locals from Verplanck or any biker guys.

They stood at the edge of the white cliff and sipped on a few cold Schafer beers from the case they had brought. Looking across the quarry, they could see the Hudson River and the hills across on the "Jersey side." They always referred to the area across the Hudson as the "Jersey side" even though Stony Point, New York, was the town directly across the Hudson from the quarry.

It was a hot, overcast day. No matter how many times they made the jump off the cliff, it was still a little scary. Scott took his shirt off and jumped in feet first. Nick yelled down as Scott surfaced and shook the water out of his reddish light brown hair made more so by the summer's sun: "Taking the safe way out, you scaredy-cat."

"No, just being smart," Scott yelled back.

Well, now it was obvious that Nick had to dive, and he regretted ribbing his buddy. As he dove out, he remembered to lock his hands above his head just before he hit the water. He went a little past vertical, and at that angle, his hands hit and forced his back to snap. Nick felt a shooting pain as he started to swim to the surface, the whole time wishing he had jumped. When he reached the surface, Scott swam over and asked, "You ok?"

"Yeah, but I tweaked my back. I'll be ok," Nick answered.

"Yeah, you are tough, you jerk," Scott said with a laugh. The two had much admiration for each other, and although they liked to rib each other, the kidding rapidly fell away when one or the other sensed the need for support.

That was a long drop—about 30 feet, they figured—and hitting the water wrong was always painful. When diving, you had to make sure you overlocked your hands above your head and broke the water with your hands leading the way so your skull would not adsorb the full impact bouncing your brain around your skull like being hit with a Muhamad Ali roundhouse. Belly flopping or going over on your back was never a fun time. Typically, the boys would dive or jump into the water off the cliffs and swim the 200 yards directly across the quarry to the three partially submerged old brick quarry buildings on the northwest side of the quarry. The cliffs on that side of the quarry were much higher, and the boys were secretly thankful that the sides of the quarry slopped back on an angle, preventing anyone from being able to jump from the northwest side.

It was a relatively long swim across, and you had to be a good, confident swimmer to make it because the quarry was very deep—300 feet in parts. Nick often thought that getting cramps halfway across would not be a good thing. As they started swimming, Nick's back started to work itself out. Once across the water, they grabbed onto the side of the building and rested. They were preparing for the next part of their journey, which was both dangerous and tiring. They had swum to the farthest building to the southwest. This building was probably a five-story building that had about three stories above water. After a few minutes, Scott asked, "You ready?" and Nick nodded. They both took a deep breath and go underwater. They entered the build underwater through a window opening and swam under the floor until they came to a submerged stairwell. They came up into the stairwell and climbed the stairs out of the water to the floor above. They had done this a number of times before, so they knew what to do, but there is no way to describe how scary the swim was the very first time and this fear of the unknown was not about being fearless because they weren't. It was still scary every time after. Once inside the building, they walked up the three flights of stairs to the top floor, where a window opened on the north side of the quarry facing the other two buildings. Someone somehow had gotten to the roof and hung a thick hemp rope from the roof dangling just outside the window. To get up onto the roof, you had to grab the rope and, while dangling over the water forty feet below, climb the side of the building and swing yourself over. Once on the roof, there was only one way down—jump about 50 feet into the water.

When they got to the window, they both looked down. "I am not doing this today, Scott," Nick said. "Not after tweaking my back off the cliff."

"No problem, Nick. I am not up for this either," Scott replied. This is where Scott and Nick drew the line, deciding it was not a smart thing to do. The truth is they never did jump from that building roof; they always made some good excuse not to. All the crazy stuff they had just done to get to this point, and they finally thought this was too dangerous. Instead, they went back down and jumped into the water from the first floor and swam back across the quarry to the cliffs. Typically, they might go onto the two-story building and jump off that, but not today. Today they had beers to drink back on the other side.

The Boys had just made it to the other side and were drying off when a long-haired guy and two girls appeared from the brush. The sun had burned off the overcast, and it was a hot, muggy day. The women proceeded to take off all their clothes and jump in the water—not caring that Nick and Scott were there. The guy sauntered over and said, "Hey, you guys got any extra beers? We'll trade you a joint." Nick and Scott were not pot smokers. Oh, sure, they had tried it and smoked it occasionally, but they preferred to drink.

Scott and Nick looked at each other and smiled. "Sure," they said in unison. "But you can keep the joint. We prefer to just drink," Scott added. The two were happy to share a few beers with this guy and his two naked girlfriends. One of the girls was long and lean and blond with small perky breasts and blond pubic hair. She had a very pretty face and a nice, round, small athletic backside. The other was a dark-haired beauty: full-figured, tan, with beautiful round breasts and large areolas. The guy was a bit older, and it turned out he had returned from Vietnam a few years back. They hung out for a little while with these three. Both Nick and Scott knew how to act cool, but they still had all they could do not to stare. It was not like Nick and Scott were used to seeing naked women freely running around, and it certainly was a memory seared into their minds. But Scott and Nick were good boys, and they had steady girlfriends. As the guy and his two friends got into some tire tubes they had brought, Nick and Scott collected their stuff, left a few more beers, and started back to the car.

When they were halfway back, Nick said, "Man, you never know what you're gonna get when you come to the quarry! Man, those girls were beautiful!!"

Scott laughed, as he was the much more experienced of the two when it came to girls, and replied, "Yeah, any fully naked girl running around probably would have looked good to you." The truth was both Scott and Nick were still steady with their high school girlfriends, and they were the type of boys who did not cheat. But, although they had steady girls, they were both still very young and naïve about women.

Nick replied, "Yeah, look who's talking. I looked over and saw your mouth opened when they first dropped their clothes." They both laughed at that. This would not be the last time the boys would encounter such experiences.

Years later, the boys saw the blond again. They walked into a strip club, and she was dancing on a small stage to Stealers Wheeler's "Stuck in the Middle with You."

CHAPTER 6
The Thirsty City

I had just returned from a visit to the memorial located next to the First Presbyterian Church in Yorktown, New York, of the Black Soldiers of the 1st Rhode Island Regiment. I had decided the visit was necessary to help shift my mindset from Nick and Scott's 20th (twentieth) century back into the history of the area during the eighteenth and nineteenth centuries. When I discovered that my namesake from the Croton area, who was a descendant of one of the soldiers from the regiment, had worked for the Bailey's, it really piqued my interest to a higher level. During my visit, I made a mental note of the dedication on the marker, which read as follows:

In Memory of the Black Soldiers of the 1st Rhode Island Regiment
Who Died in the Battle of Pines Bridge
In Defense of America's Freedom
May 13, 1781

I was about to turn my attention back to the task of filling in the historical record for the process when my friend came into my home office and said, "Jedidiah, can I fix you some dinner?" Knowing me well at this point and seeing my focus, she immediately turned and said, "I'll see you in bed later," as she walked casually back out of the room. The door slammed only slightly, but it got the message across. I faintly heard something about food in the refrigerator as I lost consciousness of what she was saying. The link to New York City, Hamilton and Burr, and the role freshwater played in New York City's future was crystallizing in such a fascinating manner that even the slamming door served as no deterrent as the tantalizing historical information quickly took priority in my mind. But this history was my interest. And no matter how mundane it might be to others, it was totally engrossing to me that my ancestors kept popping up, certainly added to my interest.

It was all about New York City. In the late 1700s early 1800s, New York City's population was exploding. Freshwater was scarce. New York City grew from 60,000 to 200,000 people between 1800 and 1830. As it grew, the little freshwater that existed was being polluted and became sparser and more unusable. Surrounded by water that was tidal and salt or brackish and unusable, the City could not survive at its current population and industrial pace. Manhattan was bound to the east and south by the East River, to the west by the Hudson, which was called the North River by the Dutch, and to the north by the Harlem River and Spuyten Duyvil Creek. The Bronx River was the only freshwater river in the New York City area, and it became polluted as the population and industry grew.

Drinking water was being provided from cisterns, wells, natural springs, and other small bodies of freshwater. In the early days, the Collect Pond and the Tea Water Spring (Tea Water Pump) supplied most of the water. The 48-acre Collect Pond was also known as the Fresh Water Pond and was located in what is now Chinatown. This freshwater water source was stagnated and filthy by the late 1700s and early 1800s. A natural spring-fed well, The Tea Water Spring was located between Baxter and Mulberry Streets. This freshwater source was similarly polluted and overused. NYC residents turned to wells, water merchants, and unscrupulous water companies for water. This is where Aaron Burr and Alexander Hamilton enter the picture. Their history was part of the corruption and underhandedness that fed the quest for political and financial power that resulted in many missteps in supplying fresh water to New York City.

There was a time when Hamilton trusted Burr; well, sort of. Although they were from different political parties, they had worked together in the past as lawyers and in introducing bipartisan legislation. Ah, yes, politicians. Burr turned the City's need for water into a scam to gain a footing in banking, which Hamilton essentially controlled. Probably well before 1799, Burr conceived his plan, which came to fruition on April 2, 1799, when the bill allowing Burr to form the Manhattan Water company as a public waterworks, which Hamilton supported, passed. What the legislature and Hamilton did not know was that Burr slipped in a clause just before final approval allowing the company to use "surplus capital," and that language essentially allowed Burr to change the Water Company into a bank. In the beginning, Burr and his company made a passable show of supplying "pure and wholesome water," but the subterfuge was quickly abandoned once the bank gained its foothold. By September 1, 1799, the Bank of the Manhattan Company opened. The ruse was over, and a furious Hamilton and his now archenemy Burr traveled into history. Burr essentially conned Hamilton into backing his plan for a public waterworks, only to form a New York public bank, the Bank of the Manhattan Company, which today is JP Morgan Chase & Co. This political gamesmanship, greed, and corruption of power at the expense of the citizens of New York set the stage for the future public water project saga that changed the course of New York City and the town to the north, whose river supplied the water.

Recurring outbreaks of yellow fever and cholera, which had started in earnest in the late 1700s, were taking their toll on the city population. Publications led with stories about "coffins lining the streets" during some of the worst outbreaks. The demand for freshwater became more critical as the late 1820s arrived. The Manhattan Company was supposed to bring water through hollowed-out logs from the Bronx River to Manhattan. With banking its real mission, Burr and his company quickly abandoned its plan of using the Bronx River. Instead, the company got all its water entirely from wells below Canal Street and the putrid Collect Pond. It sunk one deep well and built a reservoir on Chambers Street and several storage tanks on Reade and Centre Streets. The company first used horsepower and later steam engine power to distribute it to customers in wood logs bored through the center to create pipes. The system provided water to 1,400 home subscribers using twenty miles of wooden pipes. Up to 700,000 gallons per day were supplied during this period.

By the 1830s, water for cooking and drinking could no longer safely be drawn from wells in the City. The wealthy could pay to have fresh water brought to them. The poor were forced to rely on polluted water, which they made palatable by adding spirits. The Bowery Theater fires of 1828 coupled with the major cholera epidemic in 1832 resulted in the formation of a water commission in 1833 to "fix the water issues." The joint Committee on Fire and Water of the New York Common Council had previously commissioned a study by civil engineer Colonel DeWitt Clinton Jr. on November 10, 1832, to complete a study of possible new sources of water to feed the City. He was the son of Governor Clinton of Erie Canal fame. As part of this study, Colonel Clinton predicted that Manhattan would reach a population of one million by 1890, which proved to be late by 12 years. Clinton's recommendation was to create a reservoir by damming the Croton River over 40 miles north of the

City and allowing water to flow by gravity through an aqueduct to NYC. The 1835 Great Fire of New York sealed the deal.

The 1835 Great Fire of New York occurred in the middle of an economic boom and destroyed hundreds of buildings, and caused millions in property damage. At that time, New York City was a financial powerhouse bigger than Philadelphia and Boston. Recovery required financing, and the cooperation of the banks allowed for the wooden buildings to be quickly replaced by brick, stone, and mortar reinforced by steel and iron. A great need for the iron products of the Bailey's and the bricks of the Underhills of the Croton River Valley fortified their businesses. But while the fire created an economic building boom for them, it sealed their fate because the greatest public water project of the time was coming their way. The Manhattan Company Bank continued to be the only waterworks for drinking water until June 27, 1842, when Croton water flowed for the first time into the receiving reservoir in what today is Central Park.

Major David Bates ("D.B.") Douglass, a hero of the War of 1812 and a West Point engineering professor, became the chief engineer of the Croton Water Project. He was the overseer and planner for the design originated by Colonel Clinton. The Common Council formally approved the start of work on the Croton system in early 1835. Unfortunately, politics again prevailed and resulted in D.B. Douglas being fired in 1836. The political commissioners used the excuse of design arguments and delays to Fire D.B. The city politicians attributed the delays to over caution. D.B. was also having some issues with acquiring all the parcels for the project because some of the local landowners did not want to give up their farms and businesses cheaply. But it was really backroom politics and political maneuvering that caused the ill-fated change.

The Yale-educated and West Point–trained D.B. Douglass was replaced as chief engineer by J.B. Jervis, a self-taught railroad and canal engineer. Jervis only had a formal education until he was fifteen. After that, he worked on his family's farm and in their lumber business. Jervis was a Calvinist and was described as distant and reserved. His original interest in engineering and connections had landed him the job working on the Eire Canal as an understudy to the canal engineers. It was this experience and connections that resulted in his position as chief engineer for the Croton project.

In 1837, Jervis brought on Horatio Allen and Fayette Bartholomew Tower as assistants. James Renwick Jr. was the engineer and supervising architect in design and drawings. The hiring of Jervis and his assistants Allen, F.B. Tower, and Renwick by the wise men of Manhattan would change the lives of the early settlers of Croton and their descendants and alter the Croton River estuary forever.

Initially, the people in and around Croton and Sing Sing and those along the planned aqueduct route to NYC welcomed the idea of the publicly funded reservoir and aqueduct. An article in the Sing Sing Westchester Herald in 1834 by Caleb Roscoe titled "Pure Water" indicated that most of the citizens favored the Croton water project. Some local residents, however, balked at the taking of their land that had been in their families for generations. Even worse, when the work actually began, a large influx of "foreign" workers overwhelmed the area. As the project proceeded, Westchester residents turned against the project. It did not help that the locals really resented the foreign workers and the egos of the government people. The engineers and the local residents held each other in equal contempt. The engineers thought of the locals as uncouth and backward with strange beliefs, and the locals saw the chief engineer and his assistants as egotistical government workers who did not understand or care about Croton. The engineers treated the locals as unsophisticated sods, and the locals held a low opinion on the supposed talents of the engineers, often laughing at them behind their backs. Remember, despite their look of unsophistication, the locals were self-made men whose immense talents built small successful businesses and family farms in the rural wilderness. As work progressed, they described the engineers as part of the Shoddyocracy—people who get rich selling shoddy merchandise or services.

By June 1836, close to 400 mostly unskilled Irish immigrant laborers were hired for the aqueduct work. They built and lived in shanties with their families near the dam and all along the aqueduct route to New York City. By 1839 there were 3,000–4,000 laborers along the project route that reached from Croton to Harlem. A once quiet and wild Croton and the towns and villages along the aqueduct route were being overrun, and the normal lives of the residents altered. The Croton "Shanty Irish" were not welcome by the old Dutch and English inhabitants. Worse, the Irish fought among themselves, divided between the Corkites after the County Cork in the southern part of Ireland and the Fermanaghs, one of the six counties of Northern Ireland. Whiskey mills sprang up as drinking on the job was tolerated and even encouraged to fill the demand of the workers. Grogshops and drinking shanties were erected, some in farmhouses. A few local farmers had turned their homes into taverns where "a drop of the creature" could be had. This created more strife among the locals. As work began and then progressed, the residents were besieged by noises, riots, and drunken brawls. It became difficult and unsafe for women to walk near the project, and some residents complained of items being stolen and their land overrun.

Despite it all, the industrious Bailey's worked on. They were running full bore and producing tons of wire and other products, keeping at least 50 workers in full employment. They focused on their work and their church. They had worked too hard since James Bailey Sr. and his sons started the mill in 1831. By 1840, at least fifty workmen were employed at the Bailey mill. It was an established business with agents selling their products in New York City and Albany and places in between. Much of their product went to New York because the building boom after the great fire of 1835 required iron. While they knew that the Croton project would change their lives, they were negotiating for fair compensation that would allow them to continue operations below the dam. They came to America to escape England and that system. They were free, industrious people who built a successful enterprise in the wilds of the Croton River Valley, and they had no thought they could not continue.

As the aqueduct project was proceeding, the chief engineer was having problems with the two major sections: the dam in Croton and the Sing Sing arch. Before he was dismissed, D.B. Douglass had selected Garritson's Mill located four miles above the Quakers Bridge for the dam's location. With project costs rising and fear of his position with the commissioners, Jervis decided to shift the dam site 400 feet downriver from the location picked by Douglass. He thought this would be a big cost saving and would win him favor with the Whig Commissioners. The landowners along the Croton River would come to regret this decision. This drastic change resulted in major design alterations and modifications. There was less bedrock in the riverbed at Jervis's new location. This forced him to shorten the waste weir and created a narrowing of the river's water over the dam. While this change resulted in a considerable reduction in costs of the dam, it created a condition that would create a catastrophe.

The original contractor selected to complete the dam portion of the project was the firm led by Stephen Clark of Albany. Clark's bid to complete the work was based on the original location. The change caused him to quit because he knew he could not make the money he was promised. The contractor team of Henry Crandall and William Van Zandt were selected for the new location at a price 27% less than Clark's original bid. This change had drastic repercussions because it moved the location to a less favorable location on the river and created pressure on the new contractor with less funds. Most importantly, it delayed the start of the dam until 1837, setting in motion a disastrous chain of events.

The project progressed. By 1841, work on the dam was not quite finished. Still, the water behind the unfinished dam had risen, and the start of the formation of Croton Lake had begun. The pent-up river flowed several feet deep over the masonry lip of the unfinished dam as the final embankment was not yet built to its full extent. It still lacked its critical vertical protection wall. Quietly behind the scenes, Douglas, the original engineer who had been replaced by Jervis, was studying the goings-on. He was convinced that Jervis had made critical mistakes, especially in moving the dam from its original location and its resulting flawed design changes. While D.B. Douglass was a stern and rigid man, he was a top-notch civil engineer. Unlike Jervis, he had studied the history of the Croton River, spoken to the locals, and believed that Jervis and crew undervalued the history of freshets in the Croton. D.B. knew that previous freshets had flooded the river. Having been a professor at West Point for the prior fifteen years just up the Hudson, D.B. was well aware of the history of freshets in the area. He knew full well the destruction caused by previous freshets when heavy rain coupled with melted snow during a spring thaw ravaged the local area. He knew well that in this area in the streams and rivers flowing into the Hudson, the snow and ice melt resulted in a rush of freshwater flowing into the receiving Hudson. Any local—and certainly this civil engineer from just up the river at West Point—knew the history of floods on the Croton and Hudson. The history of damaging freshets that occurred in the past, such as the one that occurred on Tuesday, March 10, 1818, were well known to locals. Civil engineering requires a knowledge of the history of the project area. Jervis apparently was ignorant of the Westchester Herald story published about the 1818 freshet and the great damage it caused to "two Merchant Mills owned by Gen. Cortlandt." In their desire for fame and glory, Jervis and his assistants rushed to get the dam and project completed without taking the local history into account. Since D.B. had lost his relationship with the commission since he was fired, all he could do was watch the disaster unfold.

CHAPTER 7
Senior Party at the Croton Dam

It was June 1973, and all week there were parties for the graduating class. Today was the senior party at the Croton Dam. A truly magnificent structure, the New Croton Dam was designed by Frenchman Alphonse Fteley. This spectacular dam, completed in 1906 and put in service in 1907, is described as "a hand-hewn stone structure that has a dual part natural waterfall and part stepped spillway of terraced stone." To the high school seniors, it was just a cool place to party.

The original Croton Dam project was completed in 1842 and included an aboveground 40-mile aqueduct system from Croton to New York City crossing the Harlem River at 173rd and 174th streets through the Aqueduct "High" Bridge ending at the large receiving reservoir in what is now the great lawn of Central Park. At the time, the Croton Aqueduct was one of the biggest engineering projects in the United States, only surpassed by the Erie Canal. And despite the corruption and underhandedness with which the politicians and their hired land assessors treated the landowners of the Croton River Valley, a reliable source of clean water supported the remarkable expansion of NYC. The original aqueduct was built with a maximum capacity of 60 million gallons per day. The engineers thought this would be enough water to supply the city for hundreds of years. But it wasn't long before the ever-growing population of New York outstripped the capacity of the aqueduct. Indeed, it was largely thanks to the increased supply of freshwater that the city was able to grow so quickly. The original Croton Dam was used until about 1907, at which time the New Croton or Cornell Dam was put into service. The new dam submerged the old dam, the Bailey Mill, and many farms of the original settlers of the Croton River Valley beneath the deepest part of the resulting reservoir.

The Cornell Dam is on Route 129 and is reachable from either Croton or Yorktown. Bailey Brook starts near the intersection of Spring Valley Road and Kitchawan Road and flows north to the west of Bald Mountain. Teatown Lake, constructed by Gerard Swope, also flows into Bailey Brook. Hunter Brook and Hunter Brook Road are named for the Hunter family that lived on Hunter Brook Road starting in the mid-1800s. The brook forms in the hamlet of Shrub Oak and flows south into the Mill Pond and then into the New Croton Reservoir at Baptist Church Road. Most of the original hamlet of Huntersville, located at the foot of Hunter Brook Road, was flooded by the reservoir early in the 20th century.

Nick jumped into Scott's car, and they headed first to Scott's girlfriend, Tracy's, house at the top of the hill and then to Eve's, Nick's girlfriend; she lived on a road past the Jewish colony. As they were on their way over to pick up the girls, they stopped off at the foot of the hill at Joe's Deli to get a case of beer and ice for the cooler and some wine for the girls. Nick had already told Scott the day before that they needed to go early because he promised his Mom he would stop by the cemetery in Croton and take some photographs of her family plot. She made him promise—it was important to her, and she made that clear. She worked at the Hudson Institute, a think tank located in the Croton area. Someone there had just given her a book that mentioned her family, and she was told by someone with the local cemetery that the family plot was marked on the corners by stone Bs for Bailey, his Mom's maiden name. Nick had heard stories, of course, of his grandfather and the Bailey family history growing up—a little here and a little there, but he never really paid much attention. He was too busy with sports, his girlfriend, school, and friends. But he had seen a couple of Bailey family Bibles and saw in them the names of his ancestors from around the turn of the century.

Once in the car, Nick reminded Scott about going to the cemetery again. Scott replied, "Hey, Nick. You know, I told my Mom about going to this cemetery, and she told me that we also have a family history in this area. It seems that our ancestors came from Scotland and Wales to the Ossining area and were shipbuilders and later worked on the railroad."

It was a bright and sunny, warm early June day; it was perfect for the party, and lots of kids from their school and other schools were heading to the dam for a huge party. As they wound down the small streets in Croton, they came upon the entrance to the Bethel Cemetery on Old Post Road across from the

Croton Harmon High School and Cleveland Drive (Formerly called Five Corners). They drove up a narrow drive toward a small chapel. "Cool old church," said one of the girls.

"Look at all these really old gravestones," the other added. Really old gravestones spilled out over the hillside leading from the crest of the hill where a small old chapel could be partially seen. The old part of the cemetery started at the foot of the hill, and as they drove up the steep slope, the gravestones appeared older and older. The oldest stones were at the top of the hill surrounding the Chapel. As they looked down toward the bottom of the graveyard in the rear of the Chapel, they could see newer gravestones down on the flat, newer section of the cemetery toward Peter Beet Lane and the Croton Free Library. Much of the old part of the cemetery was situated around the old Chapel, and the stones were grouped by family and bearing family names and Bible verses or bits of information about the person buried. The Chapel overlooked the Hudson River and Haverstraw Bay to the west and Croton Point to the southwest. Many prominent people from the early part of American history, including the founding fathers of Croton, were buried here. The Bethel Chapel was built shortly after the end of the Revolutionary War and is the earliest Methodist meetinghouse in Westchester County.

They drove up the steep hill and parked alongside the east side of the Chapel at the top of the hill, where the ground flattened out. "Any idea where the graves are?" Scott asked.

"My mom indicated they were not far from the chapel," replied Nick. "How about we split up and head out from the chapel in different directions?"

"Remember, look for stones on the ground labeled B." After about five minutes of walking through the cemetery, Eve found the plot just east of the Chapel. There among the old stones were four B stone markers surrounding several very old gravestones. Within the area marked by Bs, they found stones for Joseph (born 1817, died 1884) and his wife, Phebe Bailey; John and Susan Bailey; James Bailey; Henry (Joseph's son); and others. Curiously, off to the side of the plot and away from the other stones was a lone stone that was older than the rest. It was so old that the writing on the front was worn away. The group stood in front of this grave, and Scott mused out loud, "This is interesting. Clearly, this is an older stone; it's made of a different material than the rest." It was very old red sandstone.

For some reason, Scott was drawn to the stone and the mystery it represented. "Whose could this be, and why is it off by itself, almost in a place of honor?" He said almost to no one. They stood together for some time, pondering the grave marked by the now blank red sandstone marker. Soon Scott's mood lifted as he remembered the party, and he turned and loudly said, "Hey, let's go! It's party time."

When they left the cemetery, they drove up Old Post Road to Maple Street, where it combines with Grand Street Route 129 on the east side of the Croton River toward the park below Croton Dam Road and the dam. They were early, so they decided to take a drive across the dam to the west side. They drove along Croton Dam Road and onto Blinn Road and the Teatown Lake Reservation. As they drove by, Nick noticed a sign for Bailey Brook and Cove and thought how he had spent his entire life in this area and knew nothing of his family's history. They drove past a small brook and cove just west of signs for the Teatown Reservation. His mind began to wonder. His Mom said the family started some kind of business here in the 1800s. They left England and wound up in Croton. As they drove along the road, he looked at the steep topography rising up on one side and falling steeply toward the River below and wondered how difficult life must have been here in the 1800s. "Imagine getting around here without cars. Farming here. Always going up and down these slopes," Nick blurted out. As they rode, they could see the tell-tale rock stone walls that were used to mark fields or property lines—rocks collected as the ground was cleared and used to shape walls now just seemingly weaving aimlessly through the woods and up and down slopes until they vanished into the distance.

The area has changed considerably over time as events overtook the land. Obviously, there were people working the land in the distant past, but now most of those farms were under the water of the reservoir created by the dam. Nick later found out that a 1718 census counted 91 inhabitants in the Croton, including Dutch settlers and English Quakers. The early settlers were farmers or worked on the mills that were developing along the Croton River. Others were involved with trade and sailing as the Hudson River was the main artery to New York City to the south and Albany to the north. During the 1800s, farming, cattle, shipping, shipbuilding, and flour and brick manufacturing were the main livelihoods until the construction of the railroad and the Croton dams, and the aqueduct. The construction of the dam and the aqueduct were the preeminent events that changed Croton and the people who lived there. It changed the landscape and brought an instantaneous influx of a very large number of mostly Irish at first and then German and Italian immigrants. The influx of dam and aqueduct workers significantly increased the population of the village and the surrounding areas so that by the time of its incorporation in 1898, the village's population had grown to 1,000 and to over 1,700 in the early 1900s. During the time of the building of the dam and railroad in the 1830s–1840 period, there were easily that many temporary workers in the area that months before had less than a hundred inhabitants.

This party at the dam was unique. Typically, opposing schools would never get together at such an event as it would usually devolve into fights. There was still great rivalry between schools in the 1970s. But this party was different. The Croton Dam was a meeting place for a number of schools in the area, and because this was an end-of-school, seniors-mostly party, it was held with a whole different perception because many of the kids would be moving on to colleges with many kids from other schools. Below the dam was a parking area and a large grass-covered field that spread out toward the foot of the dam along its eastern side. There were easily 200 kids from different schools. They had music blaring and beer flowing, and people were playing games of pick-up two-hand touch football and frisbee. Kids were playing together, listening to music, and drinking. There was lots of Rolling Stones, Beatles, Crosby Stills Nash and Young, Pink Floyd's Dark Side of the Moon album, Bowie, or some Motown like Gladys Night, Marvin Gay, Isley Brothers, and, of course, The Doors.

Playing frisbee was a big thing in the early 1970s. As they were unpacking the car, Nick looked over at a group of guys and girls who were in a frisbee circle. Some of these kids were really good at the frisbee and doing tricks—behind the back, through the legs, hitting people on angles. One guy in the group was great at striking the frisbee directly underneath when it got to him and driving it straight up in the air. Another one would stick his index finger straight up and catch the frisbee just under the lip when it came, and it would ring around his finger in a circle. The idea besides the trick catches and throws was to see how many throws and catches could be made without a drop or errant throw. Down a little way farther was a frisbee football game.

At the party, the boys met up with a few kids from school. One of the boys was a friend of Nick's from the football team, Barry Booker, who also was on the wrestling team. Barry was student government president and someone who Nick always held in high regard as a teammate and person. When Nick mentioned to Barry about the visit to the graveyard, Barry indicated that he had an ancestor who was a member of the First Rhode Island Regiment, which fought a famous battle during the Revolutionary War in the Croton River area. His ancestor was one of the few survivors of that battle and chose to relocate in the area, thus becoming one of the first black freeman in the Croton area. They started to talk about wrestling and football, and Barry asked Nick what made him join wrestling. Nick recounted his story of how he wound up on the wrestling team because of his overwhelming desire to play football.

Nick told Barry that when he was a freshman, he went out for freshman football. Barry and Nick did not know each other then. He explained that how as a young boy, his Mom would take Nick to his oldest brother's football games. His oldest brother was one of the captains of the Junior Varsity football team in tenth grade. He was eight years older, which made Nick around seven years old at the time. At that time, the building that was Lakeland High School was what would later become the Lakeland Middle School by the time Nick was of middle school age. The football field was located behind the school to the northeast. Today it is the Van Cortlandtville Elementary School. The area along the west side of the field sloped up a steep hill and made for an excellent viewing area. Nick would watch his mom pace along the edge of the hill, yelling encouragement to the team and her son. Nick's oldest brother was a good football player, and this scene and the larger-than-life football players made an impression on Nick as he intently watched the plays. He knew he could not wait to play high school football. A few years later, an older cousin, Bert Kelly, was a star running back for Lakeland. His cousin inspired Nick even more.

Nick's mother, Blanche (Bailey) McCarthy, was a spitfire. She always told her boys they could do anything, become anything they wanted as long as they worked hard and never gave up. In kindergarten, when Nick got off the bus crying because an older bully had hit him after the first day, Nick's Mom looked him straight in the face and told him that if the kid hit him ever again that Nick should hit him back harder. The next day Nick did, and the bully never picked on him again. It was a valuable lesson for Nick.

Nick's brother never made the varsity team, which angered his Mom. How could her son—a captain and starter, no less—not make the team? Such was the politics at a large school in the early 1960s. His brother went on to be a track star, and he may still hold the school record along with his teammates for the mile relay these so many years later.

In the fall, spring, and summers, Nick would play tackle football on the neighborhood field at the bottom of Evergreen Knolls, mostly with kids two and three years older. By that time, Nick was a tough kid as the lessons his Mom taught him made him so. Hockey was his favorite sport, and in the winter, he played hockey every chance he could on the lake in the Jewish colony. Nick learned how to skate playing hockey with his older brothers. They would let Nick tag along as long as he was willing to play goal. Playing goal meant kneeling on the ice with a tree limb to block shots. Every so often, they would let him play other positions, and he learned to skate literally chasing the puck. By the time he was in high school, he could skate as good backward as forward, and he was a tenacious player always on the puck.

Nick went on, "You know, Barry, when we were freshman, almost 200 kids went out for freshman football." I was this little kid, and I was not yet known to the coaches in high school. To them, I was just another skinny studious-looking kid who no one really knew because I went to Catholic school till seventh grade." I was in the "smart" classes with all the honor society kids." "Barry," Nick went on, "you remember there were so many kids and certainly not enough equipment to go around, so the coaches decided to pick the team based on two-hand-touch games." The coaches divided the kids up into teams and let them play with the coaches walking around and observing the games. "Little did I know, Barry, but the final football team was pretty much already selected before these games even began by the coaches based on the reputations of the kids as the "best" athletes—as well as size."

Nick went on to describe how he had the best two-hand-touch games of his life; he made numerous "tackles" behind the line of scrimmage; he recovered a fumble, caught a touchdown pass, and ran for another. He could not have played a better game, and as they were walking off the field, the kids on his two-hand-touch team assured Nick there was no way he would be cut.

Nick described his devastation when he saw his name on the cut list after coming out of the showers; playing football was all he had wanted since he was seven. Such is life in a big school and sports politics. Nick was an unknown small, skinny kid who had no reputation, and his older brothers did not play football. Nick knew he had to play some sport, so he went out for junior varsity soccer and played with Scott, who he was just getting to know better. When he sat on the soccer bus, he would see the kids going to practice on the football team, and he swore he would make that team next year.

Seeing how much he was upset over not making football, his older friends from the neighborhood, Eric Schrull and Vinny Nardone told him to go out for wrestling. They told him how they were on the team, and it would make him tough, even though they knew he already was. The thing with wrestling is there is no politics; no arbitrary selection by coaches on who makes the team or plays. With wrestling, it was beat the other kid, and you wrestled. Next year, Nick made JV football.

Although Nick was not used to talking about himself so much, he was on a roll now and so continued by telling the group how he later made the varsity football team. "You may remember, Barry," Nick started, "the first week of football practice in our junior year was very hot. There were about a hundred or so boys trying out for varsity, and we had long two-a-day practices." Nick went on that although he was developing a reputation as a wrestler, he was still relatively unknown to the football coaches, some of whom were new transfers from other schools into this big growing district. "I also did not know any of the seniors on the team." Nick described how he was relegated to the scrub team that was supposed to practice against the starters, made up of mostly seniors and guys like Barry, who was a starter on JV. Nick went on to describe the event that helped him make the varsity team. "On the last day of practice of the first week, it was raining really hard. The coaches decided to hold practice inside the gym. After practice, we were told to run five laps around the entire school before taking a shower."

Nick went on to describe how as he rounded the last turn of the run, he saw the top seniors look at him as he ran by. Nick had lapped most of the team and was one of the first ones finished. After he finished, he started walking back to the locker room just as the seniors ran by. Danny Tavares, the starting running back and a senior, was in a pack with starting tight end Lars Samuelsson, who also played defensive end. Lars was a big kid of Swedish descent with blond hair and an attitude. As they passed Nick, they yelled, "Hey, kid! Nobody walks on this team." Nick looked back and yelled back as they were about to round the bend in the hallway, "Hey! I'm done. I finished." That just seemed to anger these guys more, as they yelled back, "We'll see you in the locker room, kid."

Just as Nick was taking off his football shirt at his locker, Danny and Lars and a third senior bust into the room and headed straight for Nick. They pushed Nick up against the locker hard, and Danny said, "You don't talk back to seniors, scrub, and you run like the rest of us." Lars chimed in, "Yeah," and the other kid was behind them with a nasty face. Nick just reacted now. He pushed Danny back hard and said, "Hey! I told you I finished and don't ever shove me again, you asshole." Well, that lit the flame. The kids rushed Nick, but some of Nick's friends moved in, and a lot of pushing and shoving started. Just then, the coaches rushed in and screamed, "Hey! You guys are a team. What's this all about? Break it up, and save your aggression for the field." As the seniors pulled away, they turned, and Danny said, "We will get you on Monday during the practice scrimmage, scrub!" Lars chimed in, "You're dead!"

Well, Nick described how mad he was and that all thoughts and worry of not making the team were forgotten; he was going to show these guys. He looked at Barry and said, "You know, I don't think I would have made the team if not for that incident."

Nick went on that he knew at the next practice Danny and Lars would be after him, and he had decided how he was not going out without a fight. Monday came, and as Nick dressed for practice, the other juniors told Nick that the seniors were gunning for him. Nick explained how that was the final thing. He totally forgot his anxiety about making the team, a fear he had after his experience with Freshman football. He went on to the group, "You know, I played like a guy possessed, and it probably helped me make the team."

Nick described how practice started with the first-team offense. Nick ran out on the field to play defense. He was lined up as a linebacker on the left side. They were practicing the sweep play to the strong side, which was to be one of the main plays for the team that year. The play involved a guard pulling ahead of the fullback and the tailback with the ball with the tight end cracking down on the defensive tackle on that side. Nick knew this play well; he knew exactly what would happen and where each player would be. Nick had been paying attention in practice to every play. He knew the playbook, and he was an instinctive athlete. Nick could see the play as it was developing and could see a step ahead of where to be. As the play started, Nick knifed through the line between the guard and the tackle, sidestepped the fullback before he could react, and tackled the running back Danny in the backfield. The coaches ran over and said, "Hey, guys! Settle down and run the play right!" without any acknowledgment that Nick busted the play. The offense went back to line up to run the play again, all the time staring at Nick. Nick told his defensive teammates to be ready; he was going to bust up the line and leave Danny alone to be tackled. As the sweep came over, Nick described how he threw his body across the guard and tight end, taking them out hard and totally disrupting the play. Danny was tackled at the line of scrimmage by another "scrub." Nick had just started; he was on a mission now. These seniors were not getting past the line of scrimmage, and he roused up the rest of the players on his side. Play after play, Nick busted up the play, and finally, the coaches screamed at the offense and called the scrimmage, breaking the team up to practice in their units. After practice, as Nick was walking off the field, one of the newer and younger coaches came up to him and said, "You know what, we were not sure if you were going to make the team, but after today, you made it. That was something, kid. Where you been hiding?" Nick looked at the coach and said, "All I needed was a chance to show what I could do, Coach," and headed for the locker room.

Halfway through the season, during a team meeting in a classroom, Danny, who by that time was good friends with Nick, stood up, as a captain of the team, and addressed the team: "If we had more players like Nick McCarthy with the hard work and non-stop effort, we would win all our games." It was a little embarrassing for Nick; he was never comfortable with compliments.

The boys and their girls stayed at the party at the Croton Dam for a few hours before they decided to head home to their respective homes and family dinners. The boys had planned to meet back up at Pappa Bears—the local bar hangout—later in the evening. The legal drinking age was 18, and they wanted to catch a few beers at the bar to resume their fun before they met up with the girls for the drive-in movie and bonfire.

The Hollowbrook Drive-In Theater was located on Oregon Road at the foot of Westbrook Drive. There are condominiums there today. This area was the hub of the boys' existence growing up from when they were kids through their college years—more so for Nick than Scott because Nick lived closer. There were movies and parties at the drive-in and trout fishing and camping along the Hollowbrook stream known to some as Peekskill Hollow Creek. There were the somewhat exotic farm animals, including bulls and bison, in the Jamison family farm that was adjacent to the south of the drive-in movie. The animals sometimes would escape and wander through Nick's neighborhood or through the drive-in during a movie. Pappa Bears—later called Mutt & Jeffs—and the Carvel Ice Cream Stand were also at the foot of Westbrook along Oregon Road. This is where Nick would head at the end of every wrestling season for his traditional ice cream banana boat to celebrate not having to worry about making weight. Down further south on Oregon Road toward the City of Peekskill was Lakeland Acres, the famous swimming hole run by the Jamisons, where most area kids learned how to swim. These all added to the idyllic times and place in the late 1960s and 1970s in the lives of the boys.

When they were not outright sneaking into the drive-in to watch a movie, they would watch from a large hill behind the drive-in that perfectly faced the screen. Nick had watched the movies Kelly's Heroes and Woodstock multiple times at the drive-in.

Their favorite thing to do was to have a huge bonfire on the hill in the back of the drive-in. The boys would go down and turn all the speakers on in the back few rows, and the sound would carry up to the hilltop. They would make a large bonfire and watch the movie, party, and make out with their girlfriends on blankets—all still pretty innocent stuff of the early 1970s.

The next day after the party, Nick told his Mom what they had found in the cemetery. Nick's Mom shared with Nick a family tree that her cousin Bobby Gates had put together. This was a detailed flowchart starting with James Bailey Sr. and branching out through generations, including his own family. His family's history, which he previously knew nothing about, was all becoming pretty cool to Nick now.

CHAPTER 8

Hey, My Friend. One Slice for You?

Nick woke up from a deep sleep. The song "I Shot the Sheriff" by Eric Clapton played on the radio, and he heard the waves slamming the beach in the background and smelled the thick salt sea air. They arrived at Jones Beach very early in the morning as the sun was rising after driving a few hours from their hometown. It was the day after the prom, and this was their prom ritual. They had laid their blankets down on a deserted beach and promptly fell to sleep. As he awoke, Nick looked around and was astounded. It was wall to wall people, and his girlfriend Eve was in conversation with Scott's girlfriend, Tracy. When she realized that Nick was awake, she turned and smiled at Nick. "Hey, sleepyhead. I never saw you sleep so long."

Realizing his friend was not around, Nick asked, "Where is Scott?"

Tracy then chimed in with the answer, "He got up a half-hour ago and headed for the surf to do some body surfing. He said it was his way to wake up and shake the cobwebs out."

The prom was their girlfriends' prom; Nick and Scott were two years out of high school—old men, college kids. Over the years, they had been to a number of proms together: two junior proms and now this, the second senior prom. High school senior proms at that time were held at The Colonial Terrace at 119 Oregon Road, which was located between Scott's and Nick's homes. Directly across the road was Saint Columbanus Catholic school. This is the school where Nick went through elementary school and where both Nick and Scott played CYO basketball. Next to St. Columbanus was the Manor House, which was built before the Revolutionary War by the Van Cortlandt family and was known as the Van Cortlandt Upper Manor House. George Washington did sleep there and actually stayed for extended periods during battles in and around Westchester. When Nick was in elementary school, the nuns would often halt lessons for prayer when an ambulance would pull up to the house; it was used as an old age home at that time. Just after lunch, Nick was often asked to go outside and clean the chalk erasers by slamming them against the brick walls. Nick would miss about fifteen to twenty minutes of class, but the nuns/teachers figured Nick was smart enough to miss this time. When he was outside, he often gazed at the Manner House and thought about the times when this house was built. He knew it was old but had no clue of its history.

The boys were in love with their girlfriends; very much so, and they were the type of boys who were true. Of course, it was easy for them. Their girlfriends were the prettiest and nicest girls in school. The boys' senior prom was held in Colonial Terrace, Peekskill, New York, on June 23, 1973. The girls' senior prom was two years later, again, at the Terrace. They had already made plans to go to Jones Beach the next day, but prom night was for having fun. Nick and Scott were in the prime of their lives—strong, confident, and just a little drunk. They had shared some whisky in the car in the parking lot before walking into the prom. They were just a little late. As they walked through the doors with their girls in their arms, the band was already playing. Scott looked at Nick and then at the girls and headed straight for the band. As he did, he turned to Nick and said. "It's smiling time, Nick. We are going to sing the song." Now Scott knew Nick was shy, but he also knew that with a little booze in him, he would sing—and sing they could. As they approached the band, Scott went up to the bandleader and said something. The next thing Nick knew, Scott had the mike and had him singing the song "When You're Smiling"—the song the boys always sang together when they were out and having fun. It was kind of their way of setting the stage for the evening.

The early 1970s was a magical time for the boys. Just three years later, their lives would be completely different; both would split from their cherished first loves as they embarked on life's twists and turns. But all that was in the distant future. After prom, they spent a few hours at after-prom parties, got their girlfriends home at about 2 am, only to come back to pick up the girls at 5 am for the two-hour drive to Jones Beach. They got there at 7 am. They always went to field six and sometimes field four at Jones Beach. Jones Beach State Park was about six and a half miles of beautiful white-sand beach on the

Atlantic Ocean on the south shore of Long Island. They would spend the day hanging out at the beach, swimming occasionally, and body surfing but mostly resting from the night before. Most of the day was spent people watching the crowds, drinking beer, and eating the sandwiches their girlfriends made. Unless it was some special occasion such as prom, whenever the boys went out, they usually started the night at Pappa Bears/Mutt & Jeffs located next to the Carvel Ice Cream Stand. This was the local hang out for the kids from their school, and the Catholic schools in the same area of Cortlandt, and it was located near the corner of Oregon Road and Red Mill Road. When Nick was young, the bar was called The Grasshopper. During the early 1970s, it was usually smart to stay in your area when you went out to bars. Although they managed to get in fights occasionally at Mutt & Jeffs, whenever the boys ventured to other bars outside their area, the chance of getting into fights increased. During that time in this area, the rivalry between towns and schools and just people/outsiders was common.

Mutt & Jeffs was across from the Hollowbrook Drive-In Movie Theater. In the summer, it was common for the bar to be so crowded that kids hung out front and under a large tarped area on the side of the bar. The drive-in was constructed in the early 1950s. The Hollowbrook stream ran along the far side. Nick had spent much of his youth around the drive-in and the local swimming hole called Lakeland Acres. He learned to fish for trout with his oldest brother in the Hollowbrook stream and learned to swim, taking lessons at Lakeland Acres.

In 1949, Willis Jamison bought the property along Oregon Road across from the northern end of the Hillside Cemetery. He turned it into a private recreational park called Lakeland Acres, and it was a destination for the area, including a swimming pond, basketball courts, and other recreational facilities such as a smaller horse racing track. Long gone from the boys' time were the memories of the famous Peekskill riots that occurred at the Lakeland Acre property. Paul Robeson, a famous African American singer, and activist in the 1940s and 1950s was scheduled to perform at an open-air concert in Lakeland Acres on September 4, 1949. Several groups organized resistance to the Robeson's performance. The demonstrations were meant as a peaceful opposition to Communism, but the mood quickly became violent when some of the more bigoted opposition began fighting with concertgoers. One concertgoer was stabbed, and twelve people were sent to the hospital. Robeson got word and never started the concert. However, the resulting international attention motivated Robeson to complete a second concert further north along Oregon Road at the former Hollow Brook Country Club on land surrounding and including what became the Drive-In Movie. Even though the concert happened, thousands of demonstrators paraded along Oregon Road. As attendees left the concert, demonstrators hurled stones at the exiting cars and buses. Fighting broke out, and 145 injuries were reported. Fifty years later, in September 1999, a "Remembrance and Reconciliation Ceremony" took place at the site of the second concert. Meant to be a celebration of civil rights, Robeson's son, Paul Robeson Jr., folk singer Pete Seeger, who was a performer at the second concert, along with government officials, clergy, and local residents attended.

The original 1949 episode, which was marked by a combination of anti-communist and racial bigotry, was unknown to the boys in the idyllic times of the 1970s. Nick's group of friends included boys who were darker-skinned. But racism and bigotry still existed, as it does today, and during Nick's time in school, there were anti-war sit-ins and racial fights with blacks and greasers that closed the school down for a week. That humans still are bigoted based on race or pigmentation troubled Nick. Partly due to his naivete but mostly due to his nature and his upbringing, he never understood bigotry. When it arose in his own heart, he quickly fought it. Nick concluded that humans are tribal, and tribalism exists in many forms. Once or twice Nick had heard stories about the riots. His view was certainly anti-communist, but he had zero clue why people would make it about race. Nick was naïve to the perniciousness of racism as his basic love of people forbade it. Like many things in society, it made no sense to him at a very basic level, and so he easily and naively dismissed it.

On any typical night, the boys would leave the bar for some food and drive down Oregon Road toward the City of Peekskill. They either went to the Peekskill Center Diner on Bank Street, or they went to Napoli's Pizzeria. Napoli's was located a few doors south on North Division Street from the iconic Genung's Department Store with its rounded corners on the southeast corner of Main and North Division as it extended to Bank Street. Later, when they were older, they sometimes went to Onofrio's Pizzeria, which was closer on North Division Street from Oregon Road. Napoli's and Onofrio's were old-school Peekskill pizzerias and arguably the best pizza in the New York City area. What made this pizza special was that it was classic NYC-style thin crust pizza with a perfect sauce/cheese combination. Typically, when you got the slice, you would pick it up and fold it in half along the center and let the oil from the sauce and cheese drip off onto the paper plate.

On any given night, Nick and Scott would walk into Napoli's and head straight to the long counter that separated the small "dining area" from the working part of the pizzeria. Each placed $5 on the counter. There were two brothers who ran Napoli's, and one or both were always there. Nick had first gone to this place with his friend Eric Schrull, who introduced him to the brothers and to the ritual. Oh yes, there was a ritual. The ritual always went this way: Nick would go to the counter and say to one of the brothers: "Hey, my friend. How are you tonight?" The brothers would always answer, "Hey, my friend. How are you?" then follow with the question, "One slice for you, my friend?" A nod from Nick would send the brother off with a slice to the pizza oven to heat up. Upon his return with the slice placed on a paper plate, the brother would state, "One slice for you, my friend!" As they finished the slice, the Napoli brothers would come up and say again, "One slice for you, my friend?" and the affair would continue until the boys took their money off the counter.

CHAPTER 9

Abram Meets Joseph and Caleb

In 1682, Cornelius Van Bursum obtained Croton Point from the Indians of the Kitchawank tribe of the Wappinger Confederacy of Indians for a barrel of rum and twelve blankets. Historical accounts suggest that several years later, William and Sara Teller operated an Indian trading post on the point. By the 1800s, the area came to be known as Teller's Point. By the time the Bailey's came to Croton, farming and flour milling were the predominant industries in the area, and soon after, shipping and brickmaking followed. During the Bailey's' time, the point became famous for brickmaking and vineyards.

It was April 12, 1833, and it was Abram Bailey's 26th birthday. The day was also special for other reasons. Abram had been in the Croton River Valley for three years since he emigrated from England with his father and two brothers, John and James Jr. They started the wire mill in 1831, and the "industrious Bailey's," as they were known, worked day and night to make it successful enough for the rest of the family to come to America. Life in the Croton River Valley in the 1830s was centered around the Croton and Hudson Rivers and the Croton Valley. It was rugged landscape. Life was physically demanding and repetitive. The nearby town of Sing Sing, which later became Ossining, was more inhabited. The town of Sing Sing was reportedly built on a location of a former Indian Village whose inhabitants were part of the Mohegan tribe named "Sint Sinck." The name in translation supposedly means "stone upon stone" and refers to the extensive rock outcrops found in the southern part of the village. At that time, when the Bailey's from Yorkshire arrived, the Croton River Valley was dominated by farms and orchards and various mills, all leading to the small town and the other villages along where the Croton River emptied into the Hudson River.

Some of the rest of the Bailey family had come over from England in the years since 1831, and today Abram's younger brother Joseph, now 16, was arriving on the steamship Westchester from NYC. The Westchester ran from NYC to Albany, departing from the foot of Franklin Street in NYC, and made the trip to Albany in fifteen hours. Other steamships at the time left from the foot of Chambers Street. The captain of the Westchester was T. Wiswall. He had a reputation as a good captain and would often sing for hours as he captained the steamship up and down the Hudson, singing as he stood on the quarterdeck by the tiller on the moonlit nights.

Abram was born in England on April 12, 1807, and Joseph was born on December 12, 1817. Abram and Joseph, despite being part of a family of nine kids and being ten years apart in age, had a special bond. Abram had left England with his dad and two brothers John and James Jr., in 1830 when Joseph was just turning thirteen.

Standing on their farm next to a brook that crossed their land before it entered the Croton River (later known as Bailey Brook), James Sr. gazed across the big meadow. It was 7 am. He had called Abram away from his work. As the two stood next to the brook, James Sr. began speaking in his typical matter-of-fact no-nonsense way. "Abe," he started, "as we agreed, you are going to travel to the Sing Sing docks and fetch your brother Joseph. His letter said he would arrive today on the steamship Westchester. I don't know why he is coming into Sing Sing and not to Croton Landing, but so be it. You probably should leave now, as it's about seven miles." Never one to lose time, he followed up, "Take the short wagon aboon [Yorkshire speak for "above" or "over"] the bridge and drop off this order for that account we have next to the docks there. Pick up some supplies while you are there, and here is $200 to buy some boots and a good horse for Joseph. He can use one of our old saddles for now. I replaced the hames [metal pieces attached to a horse collar used to distribute the load around a horse's neck and shoulders when pulling a wagon or plough], so the wagon should be better now." He continued, "Be careful when you are crossing the wire bridge and be careful not to run over any of those addled Corkites or Fermanaghs or any other barmpots [Yorkshire speak for "idiots/fools"] down near the aqueduct."

Knowing how close Abram and Joseph were, James Sr. sent him to pick up Joseph, the youngest son. The family members were all eagerly awaiting his arrival. Abram drove the short wagon down across the Wire Mill Bridge that the locals referred to as the Dugway Bridge down the dugway to meet Joseph and bring him back to the family business. The Wire Mill Bridge spanned the Croton River. This was the main bridge that connected the central Croton Valley to the east side of the Hunter's Brook and Yorktown. Abram was driving the small team of horses and short wagon that they typically used to get supplies in Croton or Sing Sing. The dugway was the dirt trail/road that ran along the Croton River. The Mill was just above the old bridge on the east side of the Croton River. At that point in the river was a basin the locals called "Deep Hole" that was over six feet in depth. By this time, the bottom was covered with metal slag because waste material was thrown from the Mill, and environmental concerns were not an issue in the 1800s. Large schooners sailed up the Croton and anchored to a large rock along the creek's edge where a strong rock pier had been built. This is where ships were loaded with rolls of wire and various metal products to reach customers in New York City, Albany, and the villages up and down the Hudson River. The height of the bridge allowed sloops and schooners with tall masts to pass underneath. The bridge was made entirely of wood except where sheathing boards were fastened with Bailey metal.

Abram continued along the summit, under a low canopy of trees that covered the dugway. As he drove, he glanced at the long flat rocks and carpets of moss and the large rock crags on this part of the trail. As he preceded down the dugway, he saw the familiar rock walls along the Griffin and Underhill properties. He spotted a few raptors crossing the river to the trees on the other side to perch for fish swimming up with the tide; one a lower-flying sharp-shinned hawk and a couple of red-tailed hawks that were spooked by the wagon. One red-tailed hawk flew ahead from tree to tree as the wagon rambled along. Abram made the crossing of the Croton again just up from the mouth at a narrow point near the west end of Doverkill Island, where the river flows toward the bay. As he reached the other side, he noticed an adult bald eagle feeding on a fish at the south end of the tiny island. As the wagon passed, the eagle spooked and flew quickly away, leaving some partially eaten fish. Abram knew it would soon be coming back to finish the rest.

Stagecoaches and sloops were the main forms of transportation between New York City and Albany in the early 1800s. There were only eight steamboats on the Hudson River by 1815. But steamboats were the future. By 1824, daily steamboats were running in the Hudson Monday through Saturday. At that time, the main steamship line was the Fulton and Livingston with steamboats, the Saratoga and James Kent alternating from Albany and New York City every other day. In 1829 Cornelius "Commodore" Vanderbilt started a steamboat business that would ultimately become the North River Steamboat Association. This was an organization of steamboat owners that Vanderbilt organized to monopolize the New York to Albany run. Cornelius Vanderbilt had financed the construction of the Westchester, which was launched in 1832, and it charged $2 for a fair from NYC to Albany. At 230 short tons (210 tons), she was the largest ship on the Hudson at that time.

Abram was meeting Joseph at Sing Sing dock. The docks at Croton Landing and Sing Sing were two of the main points where ships came up the river and dropped off supplies and people moving inland into the highlands along the Croton Turnpike. Abram had expected to meet Joseph at the Croton Landing dock, but Joseph's letter said to meet him at the Sing Sing Dock. This was odd to Abram. How did Joseph even know about the Sing Sing dock?

After dropping off the supply order at the Iron Works at the foot of Central and Water Streets in Sing Sing across from the middle dock, Abram noticed that the Westchester had just docked. Even though it had been a few years since Abram had seen his youngest brother, he recognized him right away even though he was a mature young man now. Abram saw that Joseph was getting off the boat with another slightly older guy who had a shock of light brownish-red, almost strawberry-blond hair.

"Joseph! Joseph!" Abram called. "Over here!" The two embraced. It had been three years since Abram had seen Joseph, and although the younger brother was still thin, he had definitely grown in stature and had a mature appearance. Abram smiled at Joseph in his typical way. "So glad you are finally here, brother." Out of the corner of his eye, Abram spotted the guy with the strawberry-blond hair standing behind Joseph. "Who is this?" Abram asked Joseph.

"Ah, this is Caleb, my friend Caleb Croft," Joseph answered. "We met a year ago in the pub where Mom and Jane work, and he was talking about coming to America." It was not uncommon in the 1800s in industrial England for young men Joseph's age to be in pubs, and besides, this was the pub that their mom, Susannah, and their sister Jane worked in. "Caleb was in Sheffield visiting relatives and learning about where his uncle was. His relatives directed him to the pub knowing that his uncle, a man by the name of William Evans, worked at the Bailey Mill in Croton." Abram stopped Joseph in mid-sentence. "Uncle John…" as he looked at Caleb, "You are related to Uncle John? I mean William Evans?" Abram noted the perplexed look on Caleb's face.

William Evans was a stout, fifty-something-year-old Welshman who everyone at the Mill called "Uncle John." Why William was known as "Uncle John," Abram really did not know. Joseph went on, "We made plans to come over to America together, and Caleb has an appointment in Sing Sing where he has a job lined up. That is why I sent Dad the letter to meet us in Sing Sing where the steamboat docked." Caleb was from Scotland, and he was coming to Sing Sing to get work as a shipbuilder.

"I was told that my uncle—William Evans—works at the mill, but I don't know an Uncle John," Caleb chimed in as he shook Abram's hand. Abram flashed one of his renowned smiles, and as he took Caleb's hand, he said, "Wow, we all love your uncle—Uncle John." Abram went on, "Anyone related to Uncle John has to be special. I really never have known why we call him "Uncle John," but he has been with us since we started the Mill. My father trusts him with his life. We all do."

Besides his relationship to "Uncle John," Abram knew right away that there was something about this guy with the shock of strawberry-blond hair. He was friendly, happy, and outgoing, unlike most Scots he knew back in England. "Caleb Croft, that's not a usual Scottish name," Abram said. "Since you are related to Uncle John, you must be Welsh too," and indeed Caleb was. What Abram and Caleb did not know at their first meeting was what fast friends they would become. Their personalities meshed, and they were close in age. It was the start of something very special.

Joseph jumped in, "Hey, Abe. Can Caleb cadge [Yorkshire speak for "borrow"] a ride to where he is staying?"

The riverfront in Sing Sing at that time—the docks and the city blocks located to the east away from the Hudson—was the hub of activity as goods, produce, other articles, and cattle were brought in from the Croton Turnpike and farms around the nearby highlands to be shipped to New York City. The main road that Abram had traveled to Sing Sing connected the Albany Post (now US 9) to the Croton Turnpike (now NY 133).

The dock was not far from the Sing Sing/American Stables at the corner of

Mill Street and Highland Avenue, which was at the rear of Totton's Furniture Store. This was their first stop on the way to drop off Caleb at a boarding house. Caleb had an appointment the next day to meet his new employers—the Collyer brothers, Thomas and William Collyer. The brothers had started a shipbuilding company in Sing Sing initially for the NYC and Hudson River markets. They were part of the Famous Collyer Family. The Collyer Family was associated with many commercial activities in Sing Sing but were most famous for their shipbuilding. Eight Collyer brothers and their kinfolk had a very large part in shipbuilding and steamboat progress in both America and the Far East. They made steam, clipper, and cargo ships, as well as schooners and tugs. The brothers later, in 1844, moved their shipyard to Manhattan at the foot of 12th Street.

At the stables, Abram bought Joseph a stout horse and new boots from the small shop that adjoined the Bay State Shoe and Leather Company. A little farther down the road was the Sing Sing prison. Abram was following his father's instructions knowing that Joseph would have neither a horse nor a good pair of boots, and they did not have any extra good horses at any of the family farms. They tied the horse up to the back of the wagon and proceeded on their way to drop off Caleb. All the while, Abram and Caleb were in deep conversations about England, Caleb's new shipbuilding job, and Caleb's plans to open his own small shop. Here and there, Abram would engage Joseph about how their mom and sister Jane were. The trio took a short detour over to Sparta just south of the Sing Sing prison because this was the location of the Garrison House, the boarding house the Collyer's had engaged for Caleb. They stopped to drop off Caleb before going back north and home to the Croton River. There was a strong temperance movement in the 1830s, and although the Bailey's were not anti-drinking, they were not prone to drink much. They worked too hard and had seen the effects of drunkenness with the new flow of aqueduct workers streaming into the area. They did occasionally drink, and this was such an occasion. Abram knew that the Garrison House was also a place where they could get a drink. It was located in front of the rocky bluff near the point where the road from Sparta meets the Old Post Road or the Highland Turnpike. Even though the elder Nathaniel Garrison claimed to a judge that he did not sell liquor, it was common knowledge that liquor was available there. They continued their conversations over a drink. Abram told Caleb that they always needed some temporary help at the Mill, and Caleb was welcome to come whenever he wanted to help make money for his plans. Abram knew his dad would have no problem since this was kin to Uncle John. Plus, by this time, his dad was leaving more and more of the running of the Mill to Abram and his brothers.

After they left off Caleb in Sparta, the brothers took the Highland Turnpike/Old Albany Post Road and connected with the Croton Turnpike just uphill from Sing Sing Landing to the dugway and Mill. They had planned for Caleb to come by the following week and meet his uncle. To Abram, this was home—journeys end. According to an unpublished history by Patrick Persons, a descendent of original settlers of the Croton area, a later description identified Journey's End Road and its environs in the 1800s. "This region south of the reservoir, east of the Croton River, and north of New Castle was a bustling community of dairy farms and orchards and families interconnected for generations through marriage, church, and proximity. This particular intersection of roads (or highways, as the old records refer to them) was in many ways a hub of the neighborhood. Here were the local schoolhouse and the Methodist Church, the Justice of the Peace who attended to the residents' legal matters and also the location where each year folks came to pay their taxes."

CHAPTER 10
Abraham & Catherine;
Joseph & Phebe

He noticed her first in church when the Bailey's first arrived from England. She had glanced at him from across the pew, and he was thunderstruck. How could he not be? She was the most beautiful girl he had ever seen, and she was in this wild place. A beauty with Saxon-blonde hair to rival any he had seen in England. What he did not know at the time was how young she was: a number of years younger than him.

Catherine Tompkins was one of six children of Robert and Sarah (Maugham) Tompkins. Her father, Robert Tompkins, was born in 1784 in Croton. He married Sarah Maugham, with whom he had six children, including David, born 1814; Catherine, born 1816; Phebe, born July 3, 1817; Mathew, born 1821; Thomas, born 1823; and Gabriel, born May 1824.

One of the many blonde descendants of the John Tompkins clan, Catherine, her brothers, and sisters, including Phebe, were members of one of the oldest families in the area. John Tompkins was the progenitor of this Tompkins family in America. The Tompkins's were one of several founding families in Yorktown/Croton, a group that included the Travis's, Strangs, the Lee and Purdy families, and the Hyatts. Beginning in the 1740s, the Tompkins family carved out farms in an area of New Castle and in the area of Yorktown called Huntersville, where the Croton River met Hunter's Brook. This was the same place the Bailey's from Yorkshire began their fortunes in America.

It is believed that the Tompkins family tree goes back to Thom the Saxon, who fought in the bloody Battle of Hastings with William the Conqueror in 1066. History indicates that he was a crusader, and his heirs inherited a crest with insignia noting a magnificent fighting man. This Thom the Saxon, of Herefordshire in Old England, is the ancestor of the Tompkins who came to this country in 1635 and founded the Westchester Tompkins family when first they migrated from Fairfield, Connecticut, to live on lands acquired from William Pell in the Ten Farms Purchase in Eastchester, New York. The Tompkins were among the original settlers of Eastchester, New York, who built homes adjacent to the lands owned by Thomas Pell. These early settlers developed a set of articles in 1665—referred to as the "Eastchester Covenant"—which were a set of principles they all would follow structured around the church, Christian love, and honest work to be shared by the group. The compact that these families formed included the equal division of land, the construction of homes, sowing of crops, care for cattle and oxen, construction of fences, the establishment of an inn, education for the children, support for the minister, and an annual day in the spring for the destruction of rattlesnakes. They also set up a formal town meeting "that when we are settled, we meet each other together each other week one hour to talk of the best things."

John Tompkins was the original direct ancestor of Catherine and her sister Phebe, who settled in Concord, Massachusetts, in October 1635. It is possible that he traveled from England on the ship Defence commanded by Captain Thomas Bostock, which sailed from London, England, at the end of July or early August 1635 and arrived in Boston on October 8, 1635. However, because his name does not appear on the Defence's passenger list of about one hundred passengers, it is also possible he arrived earlier as part of the great migration from England. Some records suggest he emigrated from the north of England, landing at Plymouth before he moved to Concord. One thing is known: he was part of the congregation of the Reverend John Jones. The Reverend Jones and the Reverend Peter Bulkeley were Puritan dissenters and came to the colonies because they fell out of favor with the Church of England and were looking for a group of Puritans to lead in America. The Reverend Jones and his family were passengers on the Defense. In the fall of 1635, a handful of early settlers, including the reverend, arrived in Concord and built temporary homes for themselves and their cattle. By1636, the Reverend Jones became the first minister of Concord. However, try as they might, conditions were not suitable for the farmers. In 1644, the Reverend John Jones left Concord with almost one-eighth of Concord's population and settled in the Connecticut River Valley at Fairfield, Connecticut. John Tompkins and his family were part of that group. John Tompkins Sr. and his family, including his wife and sons John and Nathaniel, owned a home lot of 2 1/2 acres in Block No. 6, Parcel B in Fairfield Ct. The lot was off a highway now referred to as the New Post Road and just to the right of a large pond no longer there called Harvey Pond. William Heyden was their neighbor, two lots to the left (Parcel D). When tragedy struct the Tompkins family with the sudden death of John Tompkins Sr. sometime before 1661, it was William Heyden who married the widow Tompkins and moved his new family, including teenagers John Jr. and Nathaniel Tompkins, to Eastchester, New York. Together with nine other families, they formed a small settlement along the Eastchester Creek in what is now the City of Mt. Vernon.

Nathaniel Tompkins was born around 1645 in Fairfield, Connecticut. Both twenty-year-old Nathaniel and his older brother, John, signed the Eastchester Covenant drawn up in 1665 and took an active part in the affairs of Eastchester. In 1676 Nathaniel Tompkins was directed by Governor Edmond Andres to "seize all stray horses within the jurisdiction of west and east Chester that are without marks and bring them to the constable or justices of the peace". Nathaniel married Elizabeth White, who was the daughter of Nathaniel White. One of Nathaniel and Elizabeth's six children was Nathaniel, the second Nathaniel in the line, born in 1678 in Eastchester, New York. This Nathaniel married Elizabeth Cornell, and one of their children, Nathaniel— the third Nathaniel in the line—was born May 20, 1703, in Yorktown, New York. It was this Nathaniel, the third Nathaniel in the line, who moved to New Castle, New York, and was the founder of this part of the Tompkins clan in the Croton River Valley.

Nathaniel was a non-slaveholding, small-landowning, family farmer of land near Pines Bridge on Pines Bridge Road. After the death of Stephan Van Cortlandt in 1700 and his wife, Gertrude, in 1734, the manor was surveyed and divided into twenty large lots and twenty small lots. It was one of these original lots that eventually became the Tompkins farm.

Catherine and Phebe's grandfather was Amos Tompkins, whose father Nathaniel, the third Nathaniel in the line, eventually owned extensive property in New Castle near Pine Bridge. Catherine and Phebe's great-grandfather Nathaniel was an important man in the area because he was empowered to settle quitrents and charges in 1747 and was also later an overseer of all the roads in the township. He was also a fence viewer, an appraiser of damages, and later a deputy constable in 1758. A fence viewer resolved disputes about the maintenance of fences that divided land. Fence viewers assess damages from neglected or unbuilt fences, including damages caused by animals not kept on the owner's property. They are also charged with selling at auction strays that are not redeemed by the owner. Nathaniel and his wife, Mary Forshay Tompkins, had ten children, of whom Amos was the fifth. The family farm in New Castle mainly grew leeks, potatoes, corn, flax, buckwheat, rye, wheat, oats, and turnips and also maintained livestock, including steers and cows, fowls, turkeys, geese, sheep, hogs and sows, bees, and horses. Amos's older brother Nathaniel Tompkins was a Private in the 4th Regiment, New York Line, under colonel Henry B. Livingston. He enlisted on March 18, 1777, and served until 1780.

In 1789, Amos purchased a farm and land from John Watts for 440 pounds, five shillings. The land was bounded by lands owned by Henry Lounsberry, Joshua Rider, and James Fowler and partly by the south side of the Croton River. Amos Tompkins's farm extended from what is now Pines Bridge Road to Old Croton Dam Road (Route 134). It is thought that Amos is the Tompkins who established the locally famous Tompkins family burying ground. The most imposing monument in the graveyard is also one of the oldest—a red sandstone monument for Amos Tompkins (1742–1802). The oldest stone is for an infant granddaughter who died in 1797. Today, the Tompkins graveyard, which contains about 75 recorded graves, is set back from Pines Bridge Road and enclosed by a stone wall. Other family members in the graveyard include Amos's children and grandchildren, his brother Richard, and a wide assortment of nephews, nieces, cousins, spouses, in-laws, neighbors, and friends. The property containing the graveyard was acquired by the Hudson Hills Golf Club and abandoned and neglected. It is currently owned by IBM who committed to restoring and preserving it.

Abram had been over from England for a year, and the strangeness of the wild Croton River valley and steep wooded slopes were starting to feel like home. The landscape fit his rugged individualistic nature; it was a stark contrast from the dark and dank memory of his home in industrial Sheffield. He felt like he belonged here.

Abram and Catherine never communicated over that year, but he would see her briefly at church or when he would meet the Tompkins family for hunting or fishing trips. He was 23 when he arrived from England, and he did not know that she was only 15. Abram, his father, and two brothers worked nonstop over the first year after they arrived, getting the wire mill going and setting up their initial accounts in New York City and Albany as well as at the family farms. The year passed swiftly, and the mill was running smoothly. It was time for the annual autumn church gathering, and Abram was bound and determined to see Catherine. He had thought of nothing else but work and her for a year. Although she had just turned sixteen on September 1, Abram still had no idea how young she was. She looked and acted not much younger than him.

The annual church celebration was always held on the first weekend of October every fall, always after the harvest moon when the full moon is the closest to the autumnal equinox. It was a brief time to celebrate and give glory to God, a brief time-out after fall harvesting and before the work needed to survive the winter. The fall harvest celebration always revolved around church first, and afterward, everyone congregated at the large barn in the center of things near the church. Most of the town people's energy during the year went into the growing of food for both people and animals. Most worked 12 to 16 hours a day, six days a week from "can to can't." There was no such thing as a 40-hour workweek. The Bailey's also worked at their mill. This is why spring shad fishing was also important to the locals because it provided great amounts of food for the animals and people to use throughout the year. The work never stopped. At the end of the harvest, the processing of food and feed for preservation began, and work continued in preparation for the long winter. Haystacks were created and secured, and farmers moved some hay and fodder into the barn for the most severe weather. Corn was taken to the granary for storage, and all the human food crops were processed, hogs were killed, potatoes were stored, and vegetables were canned and stocked in cellars.

On the day of the celebration, after the congregation sat through the hell and damnation church service, they moved to the large barn for the celebration. The barn was one of the oldest in the town. It was one of the original Dutch barns, and when the original owner died, it was left to the church as a place to hold meetings and celebrations. The barn was a large structure and was renovated by the parishioners. One of the renovations was to add an English-style barn addition to one end of the original Dutch barn. The original Dutch structure had really tall ceilings supported by large hand-hewn beams. The overhang of the forebay provided protection to the three-foot strap-hinged doors beneath it on the north end. The original barn had three bays organized crosswise to the roof ridge—one for livestock, a central threshing floor, and a mow for hay, straw, or sheaves or as a granary. The barn had a hip-gabled roof with the rafters widely spaced, clapboard sheathing walls, and a core structure composed of a steep gabled roof supported by purlin plates and anchor beam posts, supported by stone piers below the wide plank floor.

The entry into the barn on the north end was through paired doors on the gable ends. As you entered the barn, your eyes were drawn to the large beams of oak that bridged the center aisle. The interior of the barn was supported by a heavy structural system. The mortise and tenoned joints and the pegged beams were arranged in "H-shaped" units with columned aisles along with a central interior space. The ends of the cross beams protruded through the columns and were rounded to form tongues.

Once the barn was donated to the church, the parishioners added an addition that was constructed like a traditional English barn with timber post-and-beam framing a rectangular space. The addition was added perpendicular to the south end of the original Dutch barn, and the entry doors were centered along the long north side of the structure as a main entrance from the road.

The harvest celebration was a draw for socializing, and everybody got caught up with all the gossip. There were all sorts of games and contests set up like corn shucking, fastest apple peeling, longest unbroken string of peel contests, pumpkin carving, and cooking pumpkin on the open hearth. There would be shooting contests, riding, roping, and milking contests. Of course, there was dancing and also eating as people brought dishes to share. Typically, there was pecan bisque, assorted relishes, biscuits/butter, mushroom pie, buttermilk coleslaw, pork tenderloin with apples and cranberries, goose stuffed with apples, roasted potatoes, pear spice cake, and harvest cider. Of course, the women would bring other pies and cakes, preserves, and all kinds of other foods. Everyone looked forward to the music and square dancing. Fiddle players were mostly self-taught and would play for hours, either taking over for one another or trying to outdo each other.

Abram saw Catherine on the edge of the dance floor talking to young Joshua Purdy and Thomas Hyatt; both were sons of other long-time prominent Croton families, and Catherine obviously knew them. He had heard that these three were friends. But it did not stop Abram. He had waited long enough. He marched right up to Catherine and, in his best Yorkshire accent, introduced himself: "I am Abraham Bailey," he said with a smile, looking straight into her eyes. "But most call me Abram." He tried his best to hide his nervousness as she almost took his breath away.

"I know who you are, Abraham Bailey," Catherine replied. "I was wondering why it took you over a year to speak to me."

"Well, well…" Abram stammered. She had managed to shake him slightly back on his heels, but he was not a man to be deterred, and he recovered quickly. As he was about to continue, his swagger returning, Thomas Hyatt jabbed Abram, suggesting that this new immigrant was a little too old for Miss Tompkins. Joshua Purdy quickly agreed and said, "Yeah, Bailey. You do know that Miss Tompkins has not yet reached sweet sixteen?" Again, he was back on his heels as he began to realize that perhaps Catherine was younger than he thought. "Fifteen?" he thought, and as he looked back into Catherine's eyes, he noticed the smirk on her face. She liked Abram, and that was clear; he was older and more mature than Thomas and Joshua. She grabbed Abram's hand and walked with him to the dance floor; Abram was still slightly unsettled by the potential age difference. He was also thinking that he had made enemies of Hyatt and Purdy. Despite the Bailey's acceptance into the community, many still thought of these recent English immigrants as non-natives. Had the large influx of Irish aqueduct workers not started to challenge the locals, their recent arrival from England may have been more of a problem than it was. But this was different; Abram now understood he had rivals for the most beautiful girl in the area.

Although they danced and talked most of the night, clearly smitten with one another, Abram backed away because of the age difference. It was common during that time for women to marry at an average age of around 20; for men, the average age was around 26. As the next three years went by, they saw each other occasionally after church and during annual community events, still clearly in love and using the time for courting. By the time Catherine turned 18, their marriage was a foregone conclusion, and a year later, they had a son, John Bailey, born September 19, 1836. Catherine Tompkins and Abraham Bailey had four children: John Bailey, born in 1836; Charles Bailey, born in 1839; Caroline Bailey, born in 1846; and Josephine F. Bailey, born in 1849. They were all born in New Castle, New York.

Abram's brother Joseph had come over to America in 1833 when he was 16. Because of Abram's courtship of Catherine and the closeness of Joseph and

Abram, once Joseph was in America, he found himself around the Tompkins family a lot. It did not hurt that Catherine's younger sister Phebe, who was four months older than Joseph, was as equally beautiful as Catherine. Joseph married Phebe Tompkins on August 13, 1841, when he was 24 years old.

Abram and his brother Joseph married sisters Catherine and Phebe Tompkins. They were the daughters of Robert and Sarah Tompkins and a second cousin of Daniel Tompkins, who was the vice president in 1817 under James Monroe. It was not the last time that two Bailey brothers would marry two sisters.

The Tompkins were freeholders because they owned title to their land. They were probably originally tenant farmers who moved north to the banks of the Croton River when the land came up for sale. The area was still quite wild, had a great reputation for being fertile, and it had access to the Hudson River (paraphrased from a quote by Chris Tompkins during an interview for a local historical article). By 1820, various Tompkins families owned some 1,500 acres. That part of Van Cortlandt Manor was known as the Middle District or Hanover. Settlement began after Van Cortlandt's death in 1700. Early European settlers like the Tompkins and other English, Dutch, French Huguenots, and Quakers who were previously tenants from neighboring areas purchased the land.

Although occupied by only a few hundred people, Huntersville became a thriving community, home to industry as well as farming. The Bailey Wire Mill was just one of the multiple mills that sprung up along the banks of the Croton along with the brickyards and orchards near Croton Point. The covered wooden Wire Mill Bridge, or Dugway Bridge, spanned the Croton River, connecting the central Croton Valley to the east side of Hunter's Brook and Yorktown. According to Chris Tompkins, author of Croton Dams & Aqueduct, "It was a coherent community, the Croton Dam project and the water that eventually flooded the area to create the reservoir for water for Gotham destroyed most of its fabric."

CHAPTER 11
Runaway Apprentice

The following ad was posted in the Hudson River Chronicle on February 19, 1838 and ran for two weeks.

"Runaway – From the subscribers

Robert Simpson aged around 19 years, bound apprentice to the undersigned, to learn to draw wire. All persons are hereby forbid harboring, employing, or trusting him on our account, under penalty of law in such case made and provided

John & Abram Bailey
Croton Wire Works, Feb. 19th, 1838."

Apprenticeship came to American soil by way of England, which brought the practice of indenture and the system of master-apprentice relationships. Being bound in an apprenticeship referred to indentured service in exchange for room and board, some clothing, food, some compensation, and extensive training in a craft. While the Thirteenth Amendment to the U.S. Constitution in 1865 formally ended involuntary servitude, the boundary line between involuntary and voluntary contracts was still an issue in 1830s New York, especially in regard to an apprenticeship. Immigrants coming to America from England and other European countries brought with them the practice of indenture and the system of master-apprentice relationships.

The Bailey boys came over with their father to start the wire mill in 1830. By 1838, their father, James Sr., was 67, and the past eight years—starting with the immigration to America followed by non-stop work—had taken its toll. By

1838, James Sr. had given most of the control of mill operations to his sons John and Abram. John being the oldest, he of course, had more say in the business, but because of Abram's nature, many of the decisions were typically his. Robert Simpson had come to the Bailey's as a recent immigrant to the five points section in New York City. He signed an indenture with the Bailey's as follows:

"Know all men that I, Robert Simpson, with the Consent of William Simpson, of 5 Cross Street, New York and recently of West Yorkshire, England unto whose custody and care at whose charge I was brought over out of England into New York, does bind myself as an apprentice for six years to serve James Bailey, Senior of Huntsville, his sons, and their heirs and assigns in all manner of lawful employ unto the full extent of six years beginning the 29 day of Sept 1837. And the said Bailey doth condition to find the said Simpson food, drink & clothing fitting such an apprentice and at the end of this time one new suite of apparel and forty shillings in money: subscribed this 28, October 1837."

Simpson was older than most indentured apprentices; at that time, most apprentices were 14 years of age or younger. The apprenticeship system at that time provided for formal indentures or contracts, in which young people were legally bound to labor for a set number of years in given trade or occupation, and in return for their service they would receive trade or occupation instruction and tutelage from their master. Although rare, some ran away from their contracts either from the dislike of their chosen trade or because of a disagreement with the masters.

John came to Abram first thing in the morning to tell him that Robert had run away, and John was angry. "Abram," John started, "I wrote this to go into the paper. That ungrateful hornswoggler, foozler." It was rare for John to be so animated and so angry, and he never cursed like that. But he ranted on to Abram, "You know we gave this guy an opportunity—took him out of the five-points neighborhood at the request of Isaac Varian for helping us set up our accounts in NYC. Ever since Varian lost the mayor's election, his people have no commitment."

"Well," Abram said, "that's what you get playing with democrat politicians. The Whigs are not really any better. That's what's so great about where we live; we are free to work in this beautiful, wild place with little political nonsense around. The fruits of our labor, you know."

By the mid to late 1830s, their father had given more and more control of the operations over to John and Abram, and by 1838, the two brothers were basically in charge. The mill was humming, but the dam and aqueduct were coming, and they knew things would not be the same. But the plan was always to move the mill once the dam was completed. They were in negotiations with the NYC water commission men and had hoped that doing favors for the democrats would pay off. Not that they liked the democrats at all; they did not like politicians, period. The Bailey's were not political but were smart enough to know how things worked.

Isaac Varian was a prominent Democrat and led the infamous Tammany from 1835 until 1842 and was the NYC mayor from 1839–1841. He first ran for mayor in 1838 but lost by a little over 500 votes to the Whig Aaron Clark. Varian accused the Whigs of voter fraud and intimidation. Varian later won the mayoral election using overt voting fraud, the outcome of which changed voter registration rules. In a strange twist of fate to this story, Mayor Varian retired to Peekskill, and his ancestors lived in the neighborhood that intertwines in the Bailey history. The Society of St. Tammany, which was also called the Columbian Order, was founded somewhere around 1786 or 1789. The organization's founders took the name from Tamamend, legendary Indian chief of the Delaware Tribe. It was essentially a political organization and had titles and rituals based loosely on Native American names and customs. The leader of Tammany was known as the "Grand Sachem," and the club's headquarters was known as "the wigwam." By the late 1790s, Aaron Burr controlled Tammany and helped turn it into a political force. By Varian's time, it was the Democratic Party political machine controlling New York City and New York State politics, and it controlled the Democratic Party nominations and political patronage in NYC. Tammany Hall was an engine for graft and political corruption and is most famous for the time when the Scottish Quaker William "Boss" Tweed ran things in the 1860s during the height of corruption in NYC.

Isaac Varian had land in nearby Peekskill and was known to the Bailey's as early as 1831, when they started the iron mill and when he was in the New York State Legislature. Varian operated a grist mill near Oregon Road and Root Lane in Cortlandt.

By 1835, they often dealt with him because his contacts helped pave the way for the considerable amount of Bailey product used in New York City after the

Great Fire. Varian controlled the political patronage in New York. The Bailey's knew this game from England and reluctantly made the proper connections, including Varian, to sell their products.

"You know, John, I am not a proponent of this indentured apprentice system. I know Dad lived that in England, but things need to change," said Abram

John didn't really hear Abram and went on with his rant, his voice rising, "The gawby [Yorkshire speak for "fool"]! We could seek legal sanctions, and he could go to prison. He knew the deal, Abram, and he agreed to it. At the end of the agreed time period, he would become free to go his own way or stay with us for full wages for his work."

Abram, now getting a little heated himself, began, "You know, John, bound apprenticeship is changing, and the unions in NYC are leading the way. I certainly have my issues with unions, but I want this to be the last!"

Finally, John—seeing Abram was now visibly upset—ended the discussion by saying as he was walking away, "Ok, Abe, but we are putting this in the paper, and your name is going on it. We had a deal with Varian and Robert."

As John began to walk away, Abram called after him, "You know, John, Robert was really a bad worker and a barmpot [Yorkshire speak for "idiot"]. He was never going to be good at this work. We are actually better off since he left. He was not happy; this was not for him. He is a daft apath [Yorkshire speak for "silly person"] and doesn't need to go to jail. He just needs a good braying [Yorkshire speak for "thrashing"]."

"Maybe," said John, "but this is not going to stand without our response."

Abram had given it lots of thought over the past few years. He never liked this indentured servant system, and he was bound and determined that this would be the last time they used it. He reluctantly went along and let John put the ad in the news classified.

This is what made Abram who he was and why people naturally took to him. He was a true believer in individual rights and honest labor—pay a decent wage to honorable men and your business, and you would be better for it. This wild little corner of America—the Croton River Valley—had become part of him. That is how he wanted to run his life and the business going forward. This was the last indentured servant he would ever have.

Nothing ever came of the ad, and very quickly, John was consumed with business and forgot all about Robert Simpson. In fairness to John, he came to Abram a week or so after the newspaper ad ran and admitted that he agreed they would no longer take on indentured servants. All the Bailey's were fair people, but they did not suffer people who shirked responsibility lightly. Abram heard a year or two later from one of Varian's political agents during a trip down the Hudson to NYC that Simpson came back to the Five Points neighborhood and was killed in one of the many fights that was common in NYC at that time between old-line Americanized Protestant English and the ever-growing Scots-Irish immigrants. The Five Points was an area in Manhattan where four streets—Anthony, Cross, Orange, and Little Water—converged. It was populated by mostly poor English and Scots-Irish and later Italians and eastern European Jews.

CHAPTER 12
The Garbage Truck

Nick stood on the side of Croton River Road and sniffed the cool, crisp air of the early summer evening as it rolled off the highlands. There was a faint smell of wild roses and wildflowers, and he was deep in thought. He was thinking about having read that in the early days of New York City, during disease outbreaks, people would come to the Hudson Highlands to breathe the fresh, clean, crisp air. As he thought this, he drew in a deep breath of the air and smiled. He was gazing out across the river valley and the river. It had just rained heavily during a quick passing thunderstorm. Such storms were frequent in the late afternoon, early evening in this area of the Hudson during the summer. He gazed across the river valley, watching the mist rise from the Croton River. He had seen this many times before as the moist air formed when the rain intermingled with the warmer air along the banks of the river, and off slate-gray-black rock outcrops collided with the air off the cooler water.

As he gazed at the river mist, his eyes focused on a particular black granite rock coated through the mist. He noticed some moss on the rock as its backside melded into the shoreline. His eyes caught sight of some deep purple flowers just past the rock growing farther up the bank before the shadows of the dense woods began. His eyes went back and forth, focusing on the flowers and then the rock until his thoughts returned, and he lost focus on both. The air breathes easy. He thought as his gaze drifted back along the river and the rising mist. He had smelled this scent many times, and it always calmed him, soothed him. He knew that soon—as soon as the truck was repaired—they would be back on their way and be at the garbage dump in about ten minutes' time. He thought how he would be faced with a far different smell that he also knew all too well. His mind shifted again; the dump was on Croton Point. Long ago, the government had decided that Croton Point was a good place for a garbage dump, and he never understood why. He was sure that there was some reason.

Then his mind shifted to how he had heard that long ago, the Point had a large vineyard and apple orchard. Boy, he thought, I bet it smelled really nice then—certainly not like a garbage dump. Before his mind shifted again, he was brought back to reality by Scott yelling, "Nick!"

The truck broke down on the way to the dump on Route 129 in Croton near the Croton Dam, and they were waiting for repairs. Nick ignored Scott for the moment as his gaze had shifted from the Croton River back toward the dam above. He looked at the Croton Dam and thought about its construction. The Croton Dam was truly magnificent looking. The current masonry of the dam was started in 1892 and completed in 1906. He recalled the time a few years back when he, Scott, and their girlfriends visited the Bethel graveyard in Croton before the senior party because his mom wanted him to visit the Bailey plot and take some photographs. Something about that visit stuck with Nick, and he could not quite understand why. He did not yet realize that his ancestors worked and toiled in this area and probably on the very spot he now stood. About a year before, his mom shared a family Bible with him that her brother George had. All the old photos were amazing and piqued Nick's interest in the family. His mom's cousin Bobby Gates had completed a detailed family tree of this Bailey clan. The tree showed that the family traced its roots back very far in America. One ancestor, Michael Chatterton on the Tompkins side of the family, was a freeholder yeoman in 1763. But in 1775, Michael Chatterton signed an affidavit along with 300 others proclaiming allegiance to King George III (dated April 13, 1775, White Plains, New York). The Chatterton motto was Loyal unto Death. History, however, shows that the Tompkins family fought against the British in the Revolutionary War. The Battle of White Plains was fought on Chatterton Hill, which was named after Nick's ancestor. These were strange times in America when families were divided on politics. This would not be the last time.

As his mind began to wander back to that day and the party at the dam, he heard Scott yell again, only much louder. "Hey Nick! Come on, the truck is ready, and we've got to get to the dump before it closes. We are going out tonight, man. Got some fun to have, and we are late because of the truck." As Nick jogged to the truck, Scott said, "Lost in thought again, hey Nick?" as he smiled and opened the truck's cab door for the ride to the dump. Scott was always on Nick, in a good-natured way, because he claimed Nick was always far off in thought someplace. It was true; he was. Nick's mind was never calm; it was always going.

The Croton Dam is beautiful and magnificent. This masonry dam is 266 feet broad at its base and 297 feet high from base to crest. Its foundation extends 130 feet below the bed of the river, and the dam contains 850,000 cubic yards of masonry. The engineers' tablet mounted on the headhouse nearest the spillway lists the spillway length as 1,000 feet and the total length of the dam and spillway combined as 2,188 feet. At the time of its completion, it was the tallest dam in the world.

On the way to the dump, Nick started thinking back a few years to when he first got the job on the truck. It was funny how he had gotten this job working on the back of a garbage truck. It was the first week of the summer of 1973. Nick had just quit his job with a local landscaper. He had worked his butt off for a week and only made 45 dollars. That was not going to be enough for school, and he tried to negotiate for more money from his boss, who told him to take it or leave it. While it was not his nature to quit anything, he realized he could not make the money he needed for school. Plus, the boss was a real hard-ass jerk—the kind of guy who thinks being a dick to people makes him tough. So, he told his boss he had to quit. He started to hitch-hike home. He was half upset that he had taken a job for so little money and half upset that he was quitting something. It was not a friendly goodbye, but he made it out without taking a swing, and in the back of his mind, he figured he had much of the blame. He started to walk home; his dad had given him a ride to work early that morning on his way across town. When he got home around 11:00 am, he heard the phone ringing as he walked down the drive. Both his parents were at work, so he flew into the house and grabbed the phone. It was Scott. "Hey, Nick. Want to work on a garbage truck? It pays 40 bucks a day, and we start Monday at 5 am. You in? I told the guy I had a buddy, and he said to bring him with." This was classic Scott. How Scott had heard about and got the job in the first place, Nick never knew.

Nick was about to ask Scott when again he was jolted back to the present by Scott saying, "Hey, Nick. Lost in thought again? What are you thinking about now?" Then Scott quickly added, "I don't want to know. Let's get this last neighborhood done so we can get home to go out and have some fun."

After the dump, the boys still had some work to do—a small neighborhood off Old Compound Road in Yorktown that included Bound Brook and Mill Pond Roads and Susan Court. This was on the way back to the garbage truck yard, and the route was planned this way. They started on Bound Brook and got out of the cab of the truck after the long ride back from the dump in Croton. It took them a couple stops, but they soon found their rhythm that they had honed working together. No words at first, just the sound of cans hitting the top of the hopper bar and the garbage falling into the truck, and then the cans set quickly on the curb. They had plans for the night, and they were late, so they wanted to finish these last few streets quickly.

The cans on the route were mostly metal, with the occasional 55 or 25-gallon drum thrown in for good measure. The boys were strong, but there is nothing quite like a 55-gallon drum partially full of garbage and the other half filled with chunks of asphalt when the homeowner repaved the end of the driveway.

They were a team—they had a system—always trying to finish quickly to get home so they could play golf or go sailing or go meet women at the bars. Because the truck had broken down, they were later than usual, and tonight was bar night. Most of the morning, they would run ahead of the truck and have the lids off the cans ready to empty before the truck got there. This was a nonunion shop—they moved because they knew when they were done, they'd get to go home to have fun.

The rhythm and approach to picking up the garbage changed depending on where they were and how the cans were set. Sometimes they were in large neighborhoods. You know the kind: street after street with houses uniformly on each side of the street. Sometimes in some large neighborhoods, they would be in there for an hour or more. Most of the time in these neighborhoods, they tended to the cans on their side of the truck unless one house had a massive amount. When they were on the part of the route with houses on only one side, the rhythm changed. The one on the "off side" would position himself behind the truck about midway along the hopper. The one on the "can side" would run over, flip the lids, and then one by one, thrown a can up in the air so that when it reached the guy behind the truck, it was already flipping upside down. The guy at the truck would catch the can in flight, and the garbage would fall out in the hopper. Then he would throw the empty can back into the air over the next can coming his way for his partner to catch and place on the ground. They used this technique usually in the morning when it was cool, and they were fresh. It required strength, coordination, and focus. Nick and Scott made it look easy.

But at this time, near the end of the day, they were using their other common technique—both moved over to grab the cans and slide them to the back of the truck. They could both take four cans, two with either hand. At the truck, they would grab one can with each hand along by the front rim of the can. They would then lift them and turn them upside down in a way that the bottom of the can would strike the bar across the back of the truck at the top of the hopper, and the jolt of the can hitting the bar was usually enough to release the garbage. When a stop had lots of cans, they were strong enough to pick up four cans with their strong arm and two with the other arm and move them quickly to the back of the truck to unload. During the course of the day, they used many different techniques. They were pros and a great team. They knew exactly how to work together when they came to each house. There was never any slack from either one; never an argument about one shirking work while the other worked harder. This never happened with these two the way it sometimes did with the others. That's why Bart McNally, the company manager, loved hiring the boys. Every summer, holidays, and any other time of the year they could, they would work.

You could fill a book about the boys' time on the garbage truck. The people who worked there were right out of a 1970s TV sitcom—or maybe a Greek tragedy. They were all characters and uniquely flawed. There was Speedy, a 40-50 something man with the intellectual level of a 12-year old. He had a speech impediment, and when he wanted to say "hustle" he would say "Hutle, hutle." Speedy was a completely bald-headed man—rare in the 1970s—and tattooed over most of his body. He had a tiger on his chest and "tex" written across his fingers. He had a half-naked hula girl on the inside of his bicep so that when he flexed, she did the hula. Speedy had one other claim to fame. He would go down to NYC to make porno films because he was well endowed, and his tattoos and general look made him unique.

There was Mitch Klartin. Mitch was a mountain of a man who kind of resemble someone from the movie Deliverance. He, too, had the intellectual equivalence of a 12-year old. He lived with his common-law wife Sweetie, who was his equal in intelligence—a small mouse of a woman with red hair who seemed like someone out of an insane asylum. They two side by side made quite the scene. They lived in a small house, and everything in it was from the garbage truck—cups, plates, silverware, rugs, couches, and so on.

When Nick and Scott first started working, they were on separate trucks. Nick worked on a crew with two African Americans: the driver, Clyde, who had his hair done in cornrows, and Mr. Martin, who said very little. On their trips to the dump after the truck was filled, Clyde would tell story after story like they do in barbershops, half of which Nick understood and half of which he did not. At the end of each story, Clyde would say, "Ain't that right, Martin?" Martin would just nod and say, "ahaw." Then Clyde would say, "Ain't that right, Nick?" And Nick would say, "ahaw." Nick liked these two, and they shared a unique relationship. Although Nick was white, Martin and Clyde had no issues because this boy worked, and that's all it took on the back of the truck to gain respect. But of course, Nick also had the kind of personality that made friends easily—strong, nimble, and happy. He was a likable guy. Nick always referred to Martin as Mr. Martin. He did not know if Martin was his first name or last name, so it was "Mr. Martin," and Mr. Martin was just fine with that. He was a 30-40-year-old wiry strong man who said little and worked hard—that is, when he was not really hungover. Martin had a really bad drinking problem. Sometimes he would not show up because he was locked up in the drunk tank at the local jail. Word was that Martin was married to Clyde's sister. Nick always treated Mr. Martin with respect, and Martin liked working with Nick because he did the job fast with no complaints. Once, maybe the first or second day they ever worked together, Clyde stopped at a convenience store in the morning so Nick could buy a drink and something to eat for the ride to the dump. Nick asked Martin if he wanted a soda, and Martin said yes. Nick looked back at him as he got down from the truck and asked what kind of soda Martin wanted. Martin said, "Millaar." Nick said, "Mr. Martin, Miller is a beer." Martin said, "That's the only kind of soda I drink," and that was that. From then on, Nick always bought a can of "Millaar" for Martin when they stopped in the morning.

Scott worked on a truck driven by Bruce and with Mitch Klartin. This was like a clown car with Mitch always the clown. He was either picking his nose and putting it on the steering wheel as Bruce was driving, or they were having diaper fights. One thing they often did was buy a quart of milk and bet Mitch he could not drink it in three seconds. Mitch always did and always proceeded to puke his guts out after. It seemed like the milk trick was a weekly occurrence, and Mitch Klartin always took great pride in the drinking and puking for any new onlooker.

There were other regulars who would work a year or two and then be gone. Bart McNally, the company manager, had red hair and a rough, handsome face. He was the guy who kept the crews in line and trucks going. Then there was

Billie. Billie, the yard mechanic, was a thin, handsome man with jet-black hair combed in 1950s style. He smoked nonfiltered Lucky Strikes and always kept the pack rolled up in his sleeve. He never said much, and he always had a cigarette in his mouth. Word was that Billie had a few different girlfriends on some of the truck routes because he was a part-time driver as well and would fill in when a driver was out sick or on vacation.

There were other characters and stories that could fill a book. One guy Nick had befriended had worked there for a short time, and one day he was not there. Nick asked Bart what had happened and was told that the cops came the night before and arrested him for murder. To Nick, he seemed like a mellow guy who would never cause any trouble. He had no place to live and slept in the barn in the garbage yard. Nick never saw or heard of him again.

Bart was always getting on the different guys and had a way of needling just about everyone. But he seldom needled Nick or Scott because, well, they were normal guys, and no one else in the yard was. It was after the second year that Nick and Scott approached Bart about them working together on a truck. Typically, the rule was that there was always a senior, experienced guy on every truck—someone who knew the routes and had worked with the driver. But because this was their third summer working on the trucks, they were both experienced, and both had worked with most of the drivers. Still, Bart was reluctant because technically, these two were only summer and holiday help, and they would both go off to school in the fall. The boys had to win a bet that involved beating Bart's team in softball to make it happen. The game was obviously won by the boys, and the next day the two were both on the same truck—hungover from partying with Bart and his team the night before. They got put on a truck with a driver they did not know. They soon found out why Bart had broken his rule and put them both on this truck with this driver. He was a young guy who was a Vietnam vet whose name was Jimmy. Jimmy was this quiet, moody guy who did not get along with most of the workers. He usually just snarled at them, and the others were afraid because they heard he was crazy from the war. There was this unspoken rule that no one spoke to Jimmy until mid-morning when he took his break. He always took a breakfast break about an hour or two into the morning. Then, after that, you were free to talk to him, but he still said very little. The boys worked with Jimmy for two summers. Jimmy had no complaints with the two hard workers he had as a crew. Over time, Nick and Scott got along well with Jimmy—as well as anyone could. The third-year working together, they worked on a truck driven by their high school friend, Nick's next-door neighbor and close friend Billy, who had gotten his truck license and, with a good word from the boys, got a job. Working on the truck was not always all work and no play. Nick and Scott had lots of fun during the downtimes or easy days. There was the one time when Scott had set Nick up to get blasted by paint. Nick was off with the large, heavy, plastic orange "running" barrel that they used to get garbage on this one street where people paid extra to get their garbage picked up from their backyards. While Nick was away filling the barrel with two houses' worth of garbage, Scott had found a full can of white paint in the trash and had it positioned so it would be crushed when he pulled the levers for the hopper blade to sweep the garbage in the hopper and into the truck. When Nick got back with the barrel, he saw Scott was about to sweep the full hopper, so he set the orange barrel down on the street and leaned on it, looking at the hopper just as Scott pulled the levers. The paint can exploded, and white paint went all over Nick, dripping off his glasses and onto the street. The two laughed after Nick calmed down, and that paint stain was on that street for three years.

Then there was the time at the Seeing Eye Dog facility where they would throw bags full of dog crap into the hopper. Again, one time a bag exploded and got all over Nick. This time Scott did not think it was too funny because Nick stunk the whole day and never did get back in the truck for the ride to the dump.

It wasn't always Nick who got the short end of the ribbing. One day Scott was way hungover, and his stomach was not good. He decided he had to take a crap. He grabbed a newspaper out of the truck and headed into this thicket of bushes and trees on a small vacant lot between two houses. Just as Scott settled down in the bushes, this old woman walking her dog started to head into where Scott was—not knowing Scott was in there. Now seeing this, Nick just started to laugh—so hard he couldn't warn Scott. The sound that woman made when she came upon Scott and the look on her face as she ran out of the woods lived with the boys forever. Then there was the time they were on the truck with Jimmy heading for the crest of a large, steep hill. Just before the hill, Nick saw Scott jump off the truck and head to a house that did not have garbage out.

Now, Jimmy had this rule: if the garbage is not out when the truck is there, he drove right by. Nick jumped off the truck after Scott as the truck disappeared over the crest and down the hill. It took Jimmy half a block to stop the truck and turn it around, and he was all sorts of mad until the boys told him what happened. Scott had seen this woman fly out of her house in a panic wearing a little see-through negligee and motioning to Scott. As Nick looked over when Scott jumped off the moving truck, he saw the woman head to the side of the house with Scott off in hot pursuit.

All Nick saw was Scott jump off the truck and head for the side of the house at a dead run. As Nick followed and rounded the side of the house, he saw this woman bent over with the lid of a can, trying to scoop the garbage back into the cans that were knocked over by dogs or other animals. Her breasts were just hanging out from her nightgown free in the wind, bouncing around. Nick's first instinct was to go help the woman, but as he started over, he wondered where Scott was. As he looked up, he saw Scott standing there looking at the woman with his mouth gaping wide open.

The woman was oblivious to all this because she just wanted to get her garbage picked up. She was saying something about how mad her husband would be if the garbage did not get collected. Nick yelled at Scott with a slight smile on his face. "Hey, buddy. Wanna give us a hand?" The boys started laughing as they headed back to the truck with the garbage, and the lady was safely back in her house. Nick asked Scott what the heck he was staring at. This was the early 1970s, and the boys were still young and naive enough that this was quite an experience for them.

Although naive, Scott and Nick were tough, strong, naturally good-natured guys. They never looked for trouble but never backed down when it showed up. They had the work ethic of their ancestors and their parents, and people naturally gravitated toward them. It's why Bart never picked on them and what made them better workers than anyone else in the yard.

Scott and Nick typically went out after work either to play softball on their team or out to celebrate something or other. Typically, they would wind up or start off at the local pub where all the kids hung out. Peekskill was the type of town where you stayed in your place. If you went to a bar outside your town, it would be to places where you were known, like some of the bars in Peekskill or out toward Mahopac or along Route 6. Once, the boys went to a bar in Buchannan called the Melt Down named in honor of the Indian Point Nuclear Plant in Buchanan. They played softball at the fields nearby at the old Fleischman's Distillery or at Lent's Cove. This bar was owned by the boyfriend of a friend of Nick's mom, who worked with her at the Hudson Institute.

Nick worked at the garbage company on and off for six years while he was home from college and graduate school. They worked every summer, during Easter and Christmas vacations, and other times. Scott, who attended school nearby, worked more. As they would joke when someone asked or kidded them about being garbage men, "Hey, it's great money, all you could eat, and everything is always picking up."

It's hard to describe what working on the garbage truck was like. There's no way to really describe it. It's hard, it's hot in the summer and cold in the winter, and it's smelly (very smelly) and grimy and well, like no other job. They worked through downpours in the summer and sleet, ice, and snowstorms in the winter. You had to be a strong man to last even one day—and not many did. It was on the truck where Scott realize how much Nick's mind would go from thing to thing, and he would often be lost in thought. Scott called Nick "The Thinker."

CHAPTER 13
Bear Mountain Disco

Halfway through Nick's senior year in college, his long-term relationship with his high school sweetheart ended. It hit Nick hard, and it hurt him. He truly loved her, but they had gone out for too long at too young an age. It was one of those times in life when a significant thing happens that changes the course of your life. The road turns, and no matter how happy or not your life maybe years later, especially in your waning years, you wonder what the outcome would have been if the other road was traveled. Nick's relationship with his girlfriend was pure, innocent love. The kind of love that lasts a lifetime but seldom does.

Scott's relationship had ended a year or two before. After their long relationships ended with their high school sweethearts, the boys moved on and met other women. Scott and Nick still hung out with a group of friends from high school. Typically, they would all meet at the local bar Mutt & Jeff's (later called Papa Bears) for a few early drinks. They would then typically head out to some other bar or party or both.

This was the disco era, and even though both Scott and Nick hated disco music, this was where you went to meet women. Of course, you had to dress the part too with two-tone shoes with big heels, tight pants flared at the bottom, and tight disco shirts with some loud pattern. Both Nick and Scott fit these clothes well.

Scott and Nick were very different from the others in their group of friends. On a typical night at the disco, the group would enter the club. Scott and Nick would head to the bar and find a place while their friends would go on the prowl for girls. They would walk around and around looking for girls to meet and usually bombing out. Scott and Nick would just head to the bar, and girls eventually came to them to escape the others trying to pick them up. On one particular night, these two very attractive blondes approach them at the bar. One said to Scott, "Hey, can we talk with you guys? We just want to escape these other guys bothering us, and we noticed you two just standing here calmly talking." Scott looked over at Nick and smiled because they both knew these two had been obviously checking them out. "Sure," Scott said. "Can we buy you, girls, a drink?" They wound up talking to these two all night and found out that they played on an all-girls softball team. The boys invited them to come to their Sunday pick-up softball game that was every Sunday at the bottom of the hill in Nick's Evergreen Knowles neighborhood. Nick wound up dating one of the girls for a few months until he found out from his brother that she was his age—four years older than Nick. It was not a common practice at that time, and Nick got the feeling from his brother when he found out that maybe it wasn't a great idea.

Occasionally, Scott and Nick would go to a different disco without the rest of the group. One particular disco was held on Saturday nights at the Bear Mountain Inn. This is where Scott and Nick usually went to dance. Probably the best way to visually describe Scott and Nick at that time would be to watch the video for Louie Prima's "Sing, Sing, Sing (With a Swing)" from the movie Swing Kids. Even though this was from a different era, Nick and Scott could do the jitterbug and often did when a swing song was played. This video closely matches the look and attitude of the boys: Scott outgoing and Nick just slightly shyer, but both very confident, athletic, and fun. It typically did not take long for Scott to get Nick to lose his shyness. Scott was more the ladies' man, with Nick not far behind. But they never ever disrespected women.

The Bear Mountain Inn was located on Route 9W at the northern end of Seven Lakes Drive at the base of Bear Mountain in Rockland County, New York. It was located in Bear Mountain State Park. The inn was built in 1913 and 1914 and opened in 1915 as the centerpiece of a park system that stretches from the edge of NYC through the Hudson Valley on what Nick and Scott referred to as the "Jersey" side of the river. It is a magnificent structure in a magnificent location and is referred to as one of the "finest examples of rustic Adirondack architecture in America." The materials used for construction were from the local area, including stone and chestnut timber. The outside was not the look of your typical disco. It had the "rustic park lodge look," but in the 1970s, the inside had mirrored walls and turquoise Formica. The original building was designed by the New York City firm of Tooker & Marsh and based on the look of the Adirondack Great Camps. The inn and park came about by a donation from the Harriman Family in 1908. To save the location from the New York State relocation of Sing Sing Prison, the Harriman family donated thousands of acres and one million dollars on the condition that the State of New York stop work on the prison and make Bear Mountain into a park. The building, described as "a rugged heap of boulders and huge chestnut logs was assembled at the base of Bear Mountain by the hand of man and yet following lines of such natural proportions as to resemble the eternal hills themselves." It was formally dedicated on June 1, 1915.

Nick's earliest memories of Bear Mountain were from 1960 when his parents took him to a ski jumping tournament—the Doerr Memorial Cup competition. The ski jumping hill was located just behind the inn, which formed a beautiful backdrop to the hill. From the 1930s on, Bear Mountain in New York State was the ski jumping center of the entire USA, and more competitions were hosted there than anywhere else.

Later, his parents would take Nick and his brothers there for a Smorgasbord held on Sunday afternoons at the inn. This was an all-you-can-eat event that Nick and his brothers loved. There was this large center table that revolved slowly, and it contained all sorts of food selections from shrimp to cold cuts to salads, pickles, and olives, and many other foods. They had a separate cutting table where a chef would slice roast beef, turkey, and pork. Another table had a diverse selection of cakes and pies, cookies, pudding, and other desserts.

Another feature of the park near the inn was the outdoor skating rink. Growing up, Nick and his neighborhood hockey team would play at this rink and try to organize games against the West Point Brats. Today, some of the old neighborhood boys still play pick-up hockey on Thanksgiving.

Earlier in the night, the boys had met at Papa Bears for a few drinks before they decided to head to the Bear Mountain disco in separate cars. As they were leaving, Scott yelled to Nick, "Hey! The last one to get to the inn buys the first round!" As they headed down Oregon Road toward the City of Peekskill, Scott passed Nick just as they passed Nick's Evergreen Knowles neighborhood. With Nick following close behind, Scott drove along Oregon Road, which changed to North Division Street, and then onto the Bear Mountain Parkway to a right onto Jans Peeck Bridge over Annsville Creek. Just as they reached the Annsville Circle just past the end of the bridge, Nick made his move as he slammed his Renault into second and then third gear around the circle as it emptied into US 6/2002, or the "Old Goat Road." Nick knew that the one who reached the Old Goat Road first would likely be at the Bear Mountain Inn first because there was no rational way to pass. The stretch of road was about three-and-a-half miles long as it started to ascend from Annsville Creek as it entered the Hudson past the national guard base at Camp Smith up past the Old Toll House and the Oldstone Inn. Gertrude Van Cortlandt Beekman is believed to have built the Oldstone. Now called Monteverde at Oldstone, it was rumored that one of the chains had been placed across the Hudson to keep a British ship from coming up the river toward West Point during the Revolutionary War. Others believe the chains were farther north, with the great chain near Constitution Island. The "goat trail" climbs 200 feet to a scenic overlook that looks out over Iona Island, Dunderberg Mountain, the city of Peekskill, and Charles Point, and then proceeds to wind around the mountain peak called Anthony's Nose, high above the Hudson River. Dunderberg, or "thunder mountain," was named by the early Dutch settlers because of the frequent thunderstorms that seemed to form over the top and barrel down the Hudson toward Peekskill, Verplanck, and Croton.

Now Nick broke out of the woods on the stretch that hugs the sheer mountain cliffs rising toward the sky on the right side and the tiny rock wall along the left edge that falls steeply to the Hudson below. The road was very narrow in this part, barely wide enough for two cars to pass, let alone trucks. Nick maneuvered along the narrow two-lane road like a professional racer as it wound sharply with twists and turns along the jagged rock cliffs to one side and a small rock wall along the cliffs that ran steeply to the Hudson below. Even though both boys knew this road well, Scott had fallen behind, as his car was not as nibble on this stretch of road. As they turned onto the Bear Mountain Bridge, they slowed to the speed limit, knowing cops regularly hang at the toll booth at the far side. Once through the toll, Scott caught Nick around the circle on the far side, and they drove up the road to the inn side by side; the bet really never mattered in the first place.

CHAPTER 14

Motts Come to Visit

Methodist Camp Meetings

(much of this is directly from Descendants of John Tompkins - Four Centuries of Pioneers, Patriots, Politicians and Plain Folk - International Genealogical Index, Film Number: 450975 by Scott Tompkins).

The Bailey's and many of the families along the Croton River were either members of the Methodist Episcopal Church or were Quakers. In the early days of the 1800s, Methodist Circuit Riders often stopped at Van Cortlandt Manor House and were allowed to stay in a corner bedroom that was kept in readiness for these traveling preachers. These included some of the more famous early American Methodist preachers such as George Whitfield and Francis Asbury.

By the 1770s, a formally organized Methodist Society existed in the Croton-Sing-Sing area. In 1777, Pierre Van Cortlandt, first Lieutenant Governor of New York, ceded to the Methodist community growing on Croton Landing a piece of property on a high knoll overlooking the Hudson River and contributed to the building of the Methodist Chapel, which is now the location of Bethel Chapel. Social life at that time revolved very much around church and home. While churches after the Revolution of 1776 were less involved in politics, they remained the center of community life. New churches were built, and old ones were rebuilt. Evangelical meetings like the Methodist Camp Meeting were enormously popular.

Every summer during August, hundreds of Methodists from the Hudson River Valley would meet in a weeklong summer camp retreat. Starting around 1800, the area Methodists would meet in Carmel and in Pleasantville, New York, but by 1805 a quiet grove in Croton became one of the new sites for these meetings.

The Bethel Chapel and surrounding cemetery were located off Old Post Road, known as the Five Corners. At first, only a small group of ardent men and women Methodists would meet for short outdoor worship during the hottest part of the summer. The Croton meeting location was in a quiet location, and it was a perfect place to meet the needs of a small company of worshipers. The powerful and influential of the Hudson Valley were part of the congregation. The meetings went on from year to year, and the numbers grew as Methodists from different villages, and different levels of society came. Pleasantville and Croton were the points most frequently visited. By the late 1820s, however, the meetings were becoming too large for most of the meeting places. By 1832, a plot of land near Croton at Sing Sing was purchased, and the start of the large Methodist camp-meetings began. The attendance of the first couple camp meetings at Sing Sing was chiefly made up of members from New York City churches and those of the Hudson River counties. Later years included those who came from Western New York and New England. By the late 1830s, annual attendance averaged around 3,000, and in some years, attendance was as high as 8,000 or 10,000.

Free time was scant for the industrious Bailey's except on Sundays and during the times of the weeklong religious camp meetings. They worked 12 to 16 hours a day, six days a week; they worked each day "from can to can't." There was no such thing as a 40-hour workweek. The Bailey's were bold men, accustomed to danger and hard work. They were self-reliant, with the raw energy needed to clear the forests, create their farms, and create the wire mill from scratch in this wild country of steep wooded hills. Over the years—and especially in the early years—the Bailey's had missed some of the weeklong meetings, perhaps attending for only a day or two when they could as they built their iron mill and farms. But by 1840, their business was established. The building of the Croton Dam and New York City aqueduct system was going to alter their lives, and the large influx of immigrants was changing the dynamics of the area. They were in negotiations with the Croton Dam Commission assessors for the true value of their business and lands. But this was also a special year. Abram's wife and Joseph's fiancé, Catherine and Phebe Tompkins had word that their cousins from Canada, the Motts, were coming, and the Tompkins clan was very excited. This group of Motts had left for Canada in 1810, and this was the first visit back in many years.

The idea of the outdoor worship was to gather and reflect on performing good deeds as a symbol of faith. It was also a chance for social contact during the sultriest portion of the year; the Croton-Sing Sing meeting spot along the Hudson was ideal. The Sing Sing campground was located on a bluff 400-feet above the Hudson in a large grove of mature old red and white oak trees with some scattered Chestnut trees and an occasional elm. The thickly covered area provided the worshiper's shade from the warm August sun and provided shelter from the rain. Cooling breezes from the Hudson came drifting through the trees, and the majestic river was in view. The surrounding area had many of the other native hardwood species, including American Hazelnut, Bitternut, and Shellback Hickory (Kingnut), which locals used for gunstocks, ramrods, and tool handles. Other hickory species were used for smoking and medicines. Most of the large variety of tree species were used by the locals in many ways. The sweet and edible nuts of shellbark hickory fed a wide range of wildlife species in the area, including ducks, quail, turkeys, squirrels, chipmunks, deer, foxes, and raccoons. The Pignut hickory was used for broom handles and wagon wheels. Black Locust was used for fenceposts and lumber for some of the bridges. Black Walnut was used for furniture. There were many other tree species, including Butternut, Buckey, Paper Birch, and River Birch, which were closer to the river. The trees presented a spectacular multi-colored canopy with bark in warm shades of tan, brown, pink, and cream. Large old trees developed gray, flaky bark on the lower trunks. Black Cherry, Silver and Sugar Maple, American Sycamore, American Plane Tree, and Buttonball Trees could also be found.

As the camp grew, it became more organized, and several permanent buildings and cottages began to spring up—although tents were mostly used. These were all laid out in avenues. One huge advantage of this location was that spring was located on the northern border of the grounds, which supplied non-stop clear, cool water to the worshipers—part of the notorious Jordan Spring that was used by many residents. A large stage was constructed in the northern center, where the regular services were held; The stage formed a semicircle around the area where the worshipers gathered. A slight slope of the land toward the stand provided a natural amphitheater. As the years advanced, the campgrounds had many improvements, including raising the spring water to a large reservoir at a central point.

As the meetings grew from the original small meetings, they became more organized by a large central committee that arranged events to be both spiritual and social. During the meetings, tents were arranged by church, city, and region. Men and women sat in different aisles. In addition to the benches around the stand, a separate area called "the pen" was set off by a rail and reserved for mourners and those seeking salvation. Traveling preachers would speak at set times during the morning, afternoon, and evening. During nonpreaching times, men talked politics, women shared recipes, and young people courted—and of course everyone caught up on gossip. There were corn-shucking contests and apple-peeling contests. The women folk would bring pies, cakes, preserves, and all kinds of food. There would be shooting contests, riding, roping, and milking contests.

Abram Bailey and Caleb Croft had become fast friends since they met when Caleb and Joseph first arrived. They did not see each other too often because Caleb worked only occasionally with the Bailey's to offset the times when sloop building, his profession, was slow. During these times, he would work with his uncle William Evans, the long-term mill employee who the Bailey's called Uncle John. So, they looked forward to their time together. After Sunday church, they often spent time with each other's families, and they also shared space when they went to the weeklong summer encampment.

This, the 1840 encampment, was neatly laid out in avenues, with about 150 tents of various sizes, about 150 in number along the pathways. As more people arrived, more tents were set up. Since the Bailey's lived so close, they were always able to get a prime spot in the campground area in the area designated for the Bethel Chapel to set up their family's and friends' tents. Besides the Crofts, the Bailey family always spent time with the large Tompkins clan because Abram was married to Catherine Tompkins, and 23-year-old Joseph was engaged to her younger sister Phebe.

The wedding of Joseph Bailey and Phebe Tompkins was to be held during next year's camp meeting on August 13, 1841. But this year, the Moses Mott family was coming from Canada to see their relatives and to visit the family graveyard started by Amos Tompkins. They came via the train from Western New York to Albany and then down to Bridgeport, Connecticut, via the Housatonic Railroad. From Bridgeport, they took the steamboat Lexington to the Catherine Market East River Dock in New York, and then they took the steamboat to Sing Sing for the meeting. Their other option would have been to come from Connecticut by stagecoach to Croton. Plans for the Hudson River Railroad were still in their infancy; it would be eight years before the rail station on River Street in Croton was built.

Moses's mother was Miriam Tompkins, and they were originally from Washington in Dutchess County, New York, just north of Yorktown/Croton. Miriam Tompkins's father was Enoch Tompkins, whose brother Amos was Catherine and Phebe's grandfather, and so the bond was strong. While the Motts were Quakers, Miriam was born into the Methodist religion. Although not always amiable, in this time, Quakers and Methodists often interacted, intermingled, and influenced one another. So it was not out of place for the Motts to attend the camp meeting.

The day before the camp meeting started, the Mott Family arrived. The Motts had made the Ferry trip back across the Niagara River from Canada and then caught a train in Buffalo to Albany. The trip took a couple of days; the same trip had taken 21 days thirty years earlier in 1810. It was the Motts' first trip back in many years to visit their relatives. The Mott family had left in 1810 for Canada, and for many years there was no news, especially during the War of 1812. Moses's mom, Miriam Tompkins, was close to the Robert Tompkins clan in Yorktown, so this visit from the children was special. Additionally, Caleb Tompkins, Miriam's brother, also had migrated to Canada in 1816, and news of him was also welcome.

The next evening, after the Motts had settled from their long journey from Western New York, Moses told the story of their trip in 1810 and their life in Canada. As they sat around the campfire, Moses began by telling how his father, Sear Mott, and his father's friend Peter Lossing brought their families across to Canada when Moses was a boy of 12 and settled in the northern part of the township Norwich on the third concession, which became known as Quaker Street. It was the wilds of Canada, and they were the first white settlers in that area. The story of their trip from New York to Canada had everyone riveted around the campfire.

Moses went on with the story.

In 1809, Peter Lossing, a Quaker from Dutchess County just north of Croton, and his brother-in-law Peter De Long visited Quaker friends in Prince Edward County in Upper Canada in Norwich Township. They purchased 15,000 acres of land in Norwich from a Mr. Wilcox for fifty cents an acre. That autumn, ten families of the Society of Friends from Duchess County, New York, including the Mott and Lossing families, migrated to Canada. These pioneers founded one of the first and most successful Quaker communities in

Upper Canada.

He told how his father, Sear Mott, with his wife and family of six children, one girl, and five boys, waved goodbye to his moms' younger brother and sister, Caleb and Sarah Tompkins, and traveled in a covered wagon from the town of Washington, Dutchess County, New York, to Canada, in June 1810. They traveled on a network of new roads and Indian trails that led through deep forests and along streams, including the Seneca trail, The Mohawk/Iroquois Trail, and the recently built Great Genesee Road. Two other families from Beekham town came with them as far as Brant County, all traveling in covered wagons. The Conestoga wagons had heavy running gear and high boxes. They were fitted with stout ash or elm hoops over which was stretched a canvas top. The wagons were drawn by four or six horses.

The trip took them 21 days on the road, and that included days of little travel such as Sundays, and when the rain was so hard, it prevented safe travel. They crossed the Hudson River at Catskill and traveled a rough, hilly road for some distance. When they came to Cayuga, New York, they crossed a wooden bridge said to be over a mile long. The country near the lake was well settled with a village near the east end of the bridge and good roads.

When they came to the Genesee River, where the city of Rochester now stands, the country was quite new with very few settlers. A number of men with horse and oxen teams had just come to repair the bridge as they came to it. The men told the families that the bridge was condemned as unsafe and crossing would be at their own risk. When the men found out that the families were heading to Canada, they tried to talk them into settling in the Rochester area instead because they said that Canada was a cold place full of Indians and hardly any settlers. Moses's father, Sear, and the rest of the men got out and walked the bridge, and checked it out top to bottom. After careful consideration, they traveled across slowly, one at a time, and safely got to the other side. They then traveled up the road a bit before stopping for the evening. The men at the bridge told them there were no houses or clearings, so they took the teams from the wagons and fed them by the road. The area was mostly oak and hickory.

As they started off the next morning, an Indian came out of the woods. He was richly dressed in Indian costume, with much jewelry and wampum. He was the first person of that kind the Mott youngsters had ever seen, and it made them keep pretty close to the old folks.

As they headed west, there were little signs of settlement, and the country was thick and wild; the road was not well maintained until about six miles outside of a village called Batavia. The fully loaded wagons could travel only 10–15 miles each day and less on the poor roads. It took them five days before they arrived at the Niagara River; they were lucky the weather was good, and the roads were much improved about two days out of Rochester when they reached the main Batavia road where it split due west to the Niagara. They were told it was an old Indian trail and that the western road led to a ferry at Black Rock for crossing into Canada. The ferry was called the Black Rock Ferry. Along the way, they traveled past Tonawanda Creek near the new Batavia Court House and proceeded to Asa Ransom's house in Erie, where they stopped to rest and water their horses. Once they reached the Buffalo Creek Settlement, they traveled along the Lake Erie beach, then inland a bit to Black Rock.

The ferry crossing was just north of the Buffalo Creek Settlement, which was the early name for the City of Buffalo at the place called Black Rock, where the Great Lake flowed into a river toward Niagara Falls. Because it was near where the river left the lake, the narrowing created a very strong, swift current. They were told that the name came from the black rock in the river on a plateau where the ferry was situated. The northern extremity of this plateau was the black rock, in shape of an irregular triangle, projecting into the river. It was about one hundred feet at the north end and extending southward and along the river for a distance of three hundred feet, gradually inclining to the southeast, until it was lost in the sand. The "rock" as it was referred to by locals was four or five feet high, and at its southern extremity, it was square, so that an eddy was formed there into which the ferry boat could be brought, and where it would be beyond the influence of the current. From this rock, teams could be driven into the boat over a connecting lip or bridge. The natural harbor, thus formed, was almost perfect. The Mott party was told that no other part of the river or shore above the Falls was suitable for crossing. The river was narrow at this point, and the landing was safe.

Before they reached the rock, the trail from Lake Erie took a sharp turn slightly north, and they came upon the Niagara River near Albany Street just north of the rock. They traveled for a short distance along this brook which Moses described as "a pretty stream which meandered through the forest to

Niagara street, where it rushed over a broken ledge of rocks pouring its crystal water into the Niagara River". The Motts were sad to note, upon our return for this trip that the stream was turned into a sewer, which empties into the Erie Canal. The ferry was just south of Albany Street at the foot of Fort Street (not far from where the Peace Bridge is today).

When they arrived at Black Rock there were only a few structures, including a hut near the brook at Albany street; Clark's boarding-house; the Porter, Barton, & Co. warehouse; and the residence of Nathaniel Sill. Three other families, two of them black families, were the only others near the rock.

This area next to the ferry was a large field that had been used by the Indians for meetings and games of sport; the south and east was bounded by a dense primeval forest. The forest spread along the banks of the Niagara River except for a few scattered huts settlers built on the Canadian shore. The principal business at that time was the transportation of salt from a dock owned by Porter & Barton at old Fort Schlosser to their warehouse at Black Rock. The salt was then conveyed to Erie, which at that time was the principal commercial port on Lake Erie, where the salt was then taken to Pittsburg.

The Porter & Barton firm had a monopoly on the transportation business on the portage around Niagara Falls, and it handled much of the trade on the upper Great Lakes. The firm had five vessels that each carried from 125 to 150 barrels of salt. The portage and transfer business of Porter & Barton grew enormously as they carried salt from Salina (Syracuse) to Pittsburgh in a complicated transportation route. The roads were slightly modified Indian trails, and the salt was shifted from one means of transportation to another - wagon, lake boat, ox-cart, rowboat, lake vessel, and riverboat were used. Salt was a major commodity as it was one of the few means available to preserve fish and meats before refrigeration. Besides the Porter & Barton boats, a few more vessels comprised the whole merchant fleet of the lake. Before the canal was built, the salt left the shores of Onondaga Lake in barrels on boats down the Seneca and Oswego rivers. The salt barrels were transferred to schooner's and shipped to the lower Niagara. Once they landed in Fort Erie, the salt was hauled in wagons to Waterford and from there floated down to Pittsburgh. The trade totaled thousands of barrels annually.

At Black Rock, during times when the wind was blowing down the lake, the vessels were stuck in Black Rock along with the boatman, captains, and traders from Pittsburg that hung out at the tavern to talk business and share their views. Black Rock was known as the great salt exchange and was a sort of commercial center for the salt merchants. In later years, the commercial and social center of Black Rock shifted to Niagara, Breckenridge, and West Ferry Streets and the nearby vicinity. When the Motts returned for this trip, the area was much changed as the black rock was dynamited away in the early 1820s to make way for the Erie Canal bed that paralleled the shore and proceeded via the Buffalo River to Buffalo Harbor. After the removal of the rock, the ferry operated from Squaw Island at the foot of West Ferry Street, and this is where the Motts made their return crossing.

Moses went on with the story: "The day we arrived at the rock, it was covered with traders from Pittsburg, captains of vessels, and boatmen, as the wind was blowing strongly from the West Southwest. The crossing here was three-quarters of a mile wide. They were told that the charge for ferriage was 2 shillings per man; 4 shillings per man and horse; 10 shillings for one horse wagon; 12 for a two-horse wagon, and twenty shillings per 4-horse wagon. The man that ran the ferry was Major Frederick Miller, who also owned the log ferry house and tavern near the ferry.

The craft they crossed in was something like a scow of about ten tons burthen, about 32 feet long by 8 feet wide, with four oars or sweeps and two men at each oar and one man with a longer sweep at the stern to steer. They started upstream close to the riverbank in the eddy and went about half a mile, then turned into the current and pulled their best. But the boat went downstream for a mile or more as fast as a horse could run before they got through the swift current. It took nearly all day to get the three teams over, one at a time, each landing at a point far down the other side. From that landing, the boat made its way back upriver close inshore until opposite the Black Rock to the wharf on the other side. On the return trip across to get the next wagon, the boat again swung out and was carried downstream to about the present Ferry Street, whence it was rowed up to the rock. These large horse-drawn wagons with their singular loads had been accustomed visitors at the ferry, and the Mott party was told to head for Douglas' store at Fort Erie, Canada. There they could purchase glass and nails for the construction of their farmsteads.

After they crossed, they headed north and came along by the Falls, where they stopped to gaze at them. Surely this was a thing of God, and Moses described their spectacular beauty and power. He told how the roar of the Falls was so great you had to yell to be heard by the person standing next to you. The water struck so hard that the mist rising from the base rose for what seemed like a mile in the sky and fell back down to drench anyone that was close.

The road along the bank of the river was good, but when they turned toward where St. Catherine's now stands, the roads were horrible nearly all the way to the Grand River, and it was the slowest part of the trip. Some small streams had no bridges; others had old, rotten ones. They would get stuck in mud holes at times and had to be pried out and have a double team pull them through.

They saw a few white settler farms along the road and came across a couple of Indian villages between Niagara and where they crossed the Grand River. They had to ford the Grand River because there was no bridge or ferry boat. When they arrived at Brant's Ford, a man rode a pony through to guide as the teams followed close behind, the water coming up to the horses' sides. They crossed very near where a bridge now stands and put up (stayed) at a little tavern that was kept by a man named Foster. At that time, on the north or northeast side of the Grand River were scrub oak plains where the city of Brantford now stands. The road was just wide enough for teams to pass, and there were no buildings or people.

At that time, they parted company with two families that were heading for Long Point, which was due south from Brantford on the Lake. They went west through scrub oak plains to meet John Yeigh in the Township of Burford about a day's journey from where they had crossed the Grand River. Mr. Yeigh was known as an honest Dutchman from the Pennsylvania Dutch.

The Pennsylvania Dutch or Pennsylvania Germans are a cultural group formed by early German-speaking immigrants who migrated in the 17th and 18th centuries to Pennsylvania and other locations in the Americas. The Motts passed several other settlers scattered around Yeigh's, which was about twelve miles of wilderness northeast from their land tract. They first settled on a farm north and west of the village of Burgessville (North half of Lots 15, 16 in the first concession) before preparing their land for development. Peter Lossing and Sear Mott and their sons went through the woods to locate and commence clearing a road and the land to build temporary shanties for the men while chopping wood throughout the winter. They believe they were the first white people to enter Norwich. For part of the winter, the Mott family helped Peter Lossing build a road between Burford and the new settlement.

Moses's brother Jacob Mott and some of his other brothers built one of the shacks. One day, Jacob went off to chop trees for the new log house. While chopping down a tree, he missed with the ax and hit his foot. Because no one was around, he painfully made his way back to the shack to bandage his wounds, all the time leaving behind a trail of blood. That evening, a pack of hungry wolves followed the blood to the shack. The wolves besieged the shack, climbing up on the roof and trying to enter through the chimney. Jacob and his brothers thrust blazing sticks at the wolves' faces to keep them from coming down the chimney and eventually scared them off.

Sear Mott had bought twenty acres of land, the ninth halves of Lots 13 and 14, Concession four, but it was some miles from where the Lossings were settling on Lot 8, Concession three. Because of the work of clearing, the Motts had to settle on a reserved lot across from the Lossings, which was the north half of lot 9, Concession four. They were the first settlers in North Norwich. The next Fall, several families, including the Lancasters, Cornwells, and DeLongs, came. In 1812, the Stovers came as well.

This land belonged to the English government. The families agreed to lease it for 20 years with the chance to purchase it at the expiration of the lease. Moses explained that when his father died, the lease had not expired, and Moses bought the land from the government when it came to market. It holds the farm he now lives on. Moses has also bought the farm where Peter Lossing settled.

Moses talked about the War of 1812 between England and the United States. It lasted for three years, and it retarded the settlers coming from the States a good deal because it was very difficult to cross the lines. Moses's two older brothers were drafted and served some time despite being Quakers. His brother Jacob served with his musket, and Enoch was a teamster. Enoch was present at the famous Battle of Lundy's Lane and helped carry the dead and wounded from the field of battle. The Battle of Lundy's Lane (also known as the Battle of Niagara Falls) took place on July 25, 1814. It was one of the bloodiest battles of the war and one of the deadliest battles ever fought in Canada. After the war, many other settlers came in from the States and other countries very fast. Moses explained that during the war, there were few settlers scattered through the woods but plenty of Indians hunting all over the place. Sometimes the Quaker settlers felt afraid that the Indians might do them harm, especially when they saw them with their faces painted in streaks of red and black, and they were acting somewhat fierce, but they never harmed any settlers or their property in the least.

The recent Rebellion of 1837–1838 disturbed the county a good deal. Otherwise, they have lived in peace. The Rebellion of 1837–1838 included two separate armed uprisings that took place in Lower and Upper Canada in 1837 and 1838. The rebellions were motivated by frustrations with political reform. Rebels made up of Canadian rebels, and American sympathizers were arrested, put on trial, and either sentenced to life in Britain's Australian prison colonies or publicly hanged.

The Motts and the Quaker settlement was 100 miles from Little York, the nearest market, where all business was transacted. The story told by Moses Mott around the campfire was the first time the Tompkins family had heard the story. It lasted late into the night, and even the younger children were still awake at its end. The resourceful Motts and the other families founded one of the most successful Quaker communities in Upper Canada.

CHAPTER 15
Caleb and Abram Go Fishing

"Jedidiah!" yelled one of my kayaking buddies as he was unpacking his gear. "Do you need any water? I have some extra," he finished. I simply shook my head, knowing I had plenty but acknowledging the thoughtfulness of my good friend. It was out of a need for both a break as well as a chance to visualize the present-day fishery that was the Hudson River that I had set up this Saturday morning kayak trip. Having already paddled the lower Croton River and into the Hudson and Croton Bay, I decide to take a trip from Cold Springs, New York, which would offer more extensive time in the Hudson. This would give me some visual context of the historical information just spit out by the "process." I had lightly scanned the data in preparation for the deep, all-consuming dive I would shortly make into it. This kayak trip would also give me a real-time view of the magnificent beauty, and breathtaking vistas of the Hudson that only a water view could give as the river traversed the highlands. It was an opportunity to visualize the places where history was about to take me.

Time and events had done little to alter the spectacular backdrops to the history that lay before me. For this kayak trip, I invited two of my closest friends because although I was no novice, the river currents, tidal variations, changing weather conditions, and heavy boat traffic in this part of the Hudson was best navigated with friends, even for expert kayakers. The variable northwest and southwest winds typically made the river very choppy, and strong tidal currents and changing courses added to the navigational hazards. On this day, the wind was nonexistent, and the river surface was like glass, with only the passing boat wakes to navigate.

The launch area was in the Cold Spring Train Station and offered beautiful mountain views of Bannerman's Island to the north and Constitution Island and West Point to the south. The scenery in the nearby tidal marsh would provide a close-up view of the fishery. We set off quickly from the Cold Springs train station launch and headed south along the shoreline, proceeding under the low rail bridge into Constitution Marsh. It was just past low tide, so the trip under the bridge would be easy with plenty of headroom and no need to duck or lay back in the kayak. Entering the marsh at dead low tide is frowned upon. Just before I steered my kayak under the bridge, I swung around to give myself a clear view of the scenery. I was presented with a perfect view of where the glaciers carved the great dome of Storm King Mountain to the west and the rock of Breakneck Ridge to the east. My thoughts immediately jumped to the evening because I knew that during this time of the year—even on this bright sunny day—it was likely that strong, booming thunderstorms would roll over Storm King down toward Croton Bay later in the day.

Just as I was contemplating the future storms and how they must have affected the people in this region historically—particularly the family that had lived on Constitution Island—one of my friends yelled from the other side of the bridge, " Hey, Jed! Watch the current when you start under the bridge. It kind of pulls you hard toward the bridge embankment as you reach the other side." At the change of tides, the current was always strong under the bridge with the narrowing of the inlet into or out of the marsh. As the current started pulling me under the bridge, I heeded his warning, steering toward the middle of the bridge and arriving safely with a rush on the other side in Constitution Marsh. "We probably have a good two, maybe three, hours before we get back here, or the water will be too high to get back under the Bridge comfortably," I said to my friends as we started our paddle down the main channel of the marsh.

Constitution March is designated an Important Bird and Conservation Area as well as a Significant Coastal Fish and Wildlife Habitat. The marsh is a 270-acre partly fresh and partly brackish tidal marsh along the eastern shore of the Hudson just south of Colds Springs. The marsh meanders behind Constitution Island, which buffers it from the main channel of the Hudson. Indian Brook flows to the Hudson River through the southern end of the sanctuary, and its unique environment attracts a wide variety of fish, crustaceans, and invertebrates, as well as amphibians. The marsh is crisscrossed by a series of channels reportedly dug in the 1830s as part of a plan for wild rice farming. After about an hour into our paddle, we had come to the far southern end of the marsh near where Warren Landing Road dead-ends at the marsh. We paddled into the mouth of where Indian Brook enters the marsh. As we maneuvered through a narrow part of the marsh heading back toward the north near the eastern shoreline, we noticed a 22-inch-long northern water snake heading toward shore with a small fish in its mouth. It did not seem to be startled by our presence as it passed just in front of our kayaks and undulated across the current. We paddled along the eastern side of the marsh, stopping briefly to chat with a few visitors on the boardwalk installed for hikers to access the marsh. We took a channel west back toward Constitution Island in search of the main channel.

The British gave Constitution Island as part of a land grant to the Dutch Philipse family, who was related to the Van Cortlandt family through marriage. The early Dutch name for the island was Martelaer's Rock, or Martelaer's Island. It played a large role in the Revolutionary War, housing some of the earliest fortifications. It was the location where a heavy metal chain was laid across the Hudson to prevent British ships from moving up the river. The island is directly opposite West Point and has been part of West Point since 1909. Because the Philipse family were British loyalists, they forfeited the island. Eventually, the island and adjacent marsh were purchased in 1836 by Henry Warner, a wealthy New York City lawyer whose vision was to build a family summer retreat. Henry Warner bought the island after seeing it during a visit to his brother, Thomas Warner, who was the West Point chaplain. Not two years later, when he had lost all of his money in the "Panic of 1837," he moved there year-round with his daughters. He dug numerous tidal channels and erected numerous dams, which are believed to be the main channels used by kayakers today. Unfortunately, due to legal troubles with his neighbors, Warner's plans never materialize.

As we exited the marsh back into the Hudson toward Cold Springs, we could hear low sounds of thunder off to the northwest. At first, we thought it might be cannon exercises at the military academy, but a quick look at the darkening sky over Storm King told us a thunderstorm was on its way. Luckily, we would be out of the water and in our trucks before this unusually early storm would arrive. It was just a reminder that the weather and winds could change quickly in this part of the Hudson.

The kayak trip was just what I needed. Spending four hours with my friends was special, but the feelings I got from the beauty and visuals of the area set me up perfectly for the work to come. I sat back down around 7 p.m. with a bourbon and my work.

The summer of 1840 marked seven years since Abram and Caleb had met on the dock when he and his brother Joseph first arrived from England. Over that time, they had become close friends. It was the kind of friendship two guys establish when they just really have a commonality in thought and habit. Caleb's family history dated from the Anglo-Saxon culture of Herefordshire, Britain, which borders the Welsh counties of Monmouthshire and Powys to the west. Caleb's mother's name was Lydia Evans, and her brother William worked at the Bailey Mill and was known as Uncle John.

Whenever they had a chance, they would get together, which wasn't often because they were both hard-working family men. Abram had been married for five years and had two sons, John and Charles. Caleb had been married for four years and had a girl and a boy. Caleb had married Hannah, a girl he had met in Sing Sing, where he worked for the Collyer brothers. Hannah was related by marriage to that family. Her sister was married to one of the eight Collyer brothers. Most of the time, Caleb and Abram saw each other at family events or events wrapped around the community or church meetings. They did not live very close to each other—Caleb was closer to his work in Sing Sing— and so it was only on certain occasions they would get to spend time together. Their families always helped each other when help was needed. There was a bond between these two. The type of true unbreakable friendship between men who went through intense times together in day to day survival—from one day to the next. When they worked together, it was always side by side. They trusted each other and always shared the workload, working in unison as a team without thought. It just was naturally so.

They seldom had much time alone anymore—not like in the early days when Caleb first arrived, and neither had married yet. Early on, they spent some time working and spring fishing together. It was during these times that they cemented their friendship, as well as at Sunday meetings and church.

This was such a time. It was the summer that both families decided to go to the weeklong Methodist retreat held in Sing Sing. After getting permission from their wives, Catherine and Hannah, Abram and Caleb had made plans to cut out on their own to go fishing together during one of the days of the retreat. Sure, they fished together when the shad and strippers were running in late April-early May—the time of Shad fishing—but this was different. For the men and their families in the Croton Valley, shad fishing during the spring was a necessity for the farmers, and it was profitable for the local fishermen. For the Bailey's, besides the times when they would attend the summer Methodist retreat, fishing and hunting were the only time they took away from their steel mill and their farms. Fishing for shad was a necessity; it provided food for the family and for the farm animals for the year. During six weeks in spring, the shad migrated 80 to 120 miles up the Hudson River to their spawning grounds—the sand bars between Kingston and Coxsackie. It was not uncommon for as many as 2,500 shad and 6,000 herring/shad to be taken from the Hudson off Croton Point during these times. Like the other farmers, the Bailey's salted shad in barrels for their own winter consumption and to feed their farm animals, and parts were used as fertilizer. In good years, they even were able to sell some. Typically, the Bailey's would use fyke or bag nets and hoop nets, but the local fishermen used the more efficient stake gill nets, which had just been introduced to the area.

Occasionally, during other parts of the year, especially in the late winter and early spring days when the weather was warm, Abram and Caleb would go fishing after the Sunday meeting. On these days, they would fish for the other abundant Hudson fish such as striped bass, white perch, and infant sturgeon. On these days, you could usually count on a good catch twice a day when the tide was "slack," filling their nets when it is ebbing or flowing. It was not uncommon to catch bass weighing from thirty to forty pounds. In Haverstraw Bay, the widest expanse of the Hudson, they would see various different kinds of fish in large numbers in the late spring or early summer sun.

But it was August, which was not typically the time for fishing, so this fishing trip was really more a time to spend together alone. Their wives knew it too. Catherine and Hannah knew how much their men needed to get away together, and, truth be told, they wanted some relief from the men as well.

Abram and Caleb snuck out quietly out of the campgrounds when it was still dark and made sure not to wake anyone. They had padded the horses' shoes to muffle the sound of the huffs, and they had their gear packed the night before. They started off for their favorite fishing spot on the southern corner of Croton Point in a spot well away from the effluent streams of the Underhill Brick Works. This was going to be an all-day affair because it would take time to get to the point from the campground, and the Croton Point peninsula juts into the Hudson River for almost two miles from the east shore. They set off to ride the approximately four miles. At the start, the road was very hilly and travel was slow, and they knew they would be back very late that night. They walked their horses out of the meeting grounds under the canopy of the various species of oak, chestnut, and maple trees that made up the grove. When they reached just past the northwestern edge of the campgrounds, they stopped to remove the padding from their horses' shoes. Luckily it was a full moon, and they did not need torches. Just then, the horses spooked and raised their front legs. As Abram struggled with the horses, he shouted to Caleb, who was near their rear, "Ey up [Yorkshire speak for "lookout"]! The horses were frit [Yorkshire speak for "frightened"] by that rattlesnake!" As Caleb looks around the horses, he sees a two-foot timber rattlesnake move slowly across the road in front of them. The snake was keeping its distance as it slithered into the thick brush and darkness. Just then, a barred owl in the tree above vocalized raucously in the typical "Ooh, ooh ahoo. Ooh, ooh ahoo." Abram said, "Ah, listen to that Ullet [Yorkshire speak for "owl"] cry a warning." Once Caleb regained his composure, he laughed. "Aye, Abram. You been in this country how long, and you still revert to that Yorkshire slang whenever you get excited."

They traveled down from the campgrounds north toward Croton Point along North Highland Avenue and then to River Road. As they turned west toward the river from the higher north-south road, they rode through an area of evergreen trees similar to those farther up the Croton River near where the Battle of Pines Bridge Pass happened during the Revolutionary War. They rode through various species of pines and fir trees, including a patch of white pines, with some reaching nearly 200 feet in height. Abram and Caleb knew that this is where many of the eagles and osprey had their nests in the "super canopy," which provides easy access to and from the nest to the Croton and Hudson Rivers. As they approached, they were reminded of this when the familiar call of the bald eagle sang out. Hawks, vultures, and bald eagles roamed the area because of the rich fishery and natural habitat. In a few months, the autumn ritual of migration of birds would start to occur in the Hudson Valley. Even the western species of hummingbird would start to appear in more abundance. These and other birds are wandering migrants that are flushed south by lessening daylight, colder weather, and a reduced food supply.

As they traveled northwest, the trees changed to more common pine and fir trees, including Pitch Pine, Red Pine, Jack (Grey or Scrub Pine), and Balsam Fir. They crossed Auser's Flats and headed toward Croton Point as dawn approached. They came upon a copperhead lounging on a rock waiting for full sun near the side of the path. The snake was about three feet long and probably a female because they are typically larger than males. It did not seem concerned by their presence, but they still kept a healthy distance; they did not want the horses to get spooked again. Abram recalled to Caleb the day a few years back when he and his brother John came upon a copperhead on the dug road, and the team of horses went crazy, almost overturning the wagon. As they crossed the Croton River east of its mouth, they saw the west end of Doverkill Island as they headed for Enoch Point. Access to the Point was over the hill along the north side of the Point. The bridge being built to support the coming railroad was known to local residents as the Kissing Bridge. Most of the people living on the Point lived in a small village at the mainland end of the peninsula. These families were mostly associated with either the Underhill brickworks or the Underhill vineyards. There was a store, a school, a tavern, a boarding house, and other facilities all on that end.

In days past, Croton Point would be free of people except for the orchard and vineyard workers in the south and the brickyard workers in the north. The small town developed at the beginning of the point for the workers. But since the aqueduct had started, hundreds of men and some families—mostly from Ireland and associated with the work on the dam and aqueduct—were everywhere. Often there were drunken men who were temporarily relieved from work because they had drunk too much or those who were not working because of a temporary work stoppage. There was often much trouble as the old religious rivalry of the Corkites from south Ireland often fought with the Fermanaghs from northern Ireland. The once quiet and reserved Croton was now besieged by noises, riots, and drunken brawls. Grogshops and drinking shanties had not reached the Point because most were erected closer to the dam and aqueduct route. So most of these problems were not on the Point. But these new arrivals also took advantage of the fishery, and thus many more people were now on and around the river and its tributaries. This was another reason they chose to fish on the southern point—on R.T. Underhill's land; it was off-limits to the dam workers. The Bailey's and Underhills were old friends even though they attended separate churches. The Bailey's had an open invitation to the fishing on the southern point because they had helped R.T. with iron and steel needs and the construction of his wine vaults. Caleb was a friend too, because he had built a special flat-bottomed, two-masted periauger sailing vessel that the Underhills used to ferry goods from their mill on the Croton River to their winery at the Point or supplies for their brick factory to and from the Croton docks.

Once Abram and Caleb got past the village and onto the Point, they traveled past the Manor Cemetery and farther along past Haunted Hollow—the Kitchawan burial ground, which many said was haunted with the souls of the departed Indians. Locals called them the Walking Sachems of Teller's Point. Caleb and Abram purposefully skipped the northwest point and Mothers Lap where the brickyards were and headed straight down Dyke Road past the lowland marshes. As they rounded a bend, the vast Underhill vineyards and orchards spread out before them. As they headed toward the south, or Tellers Point, they could see across the vast open vineyards toward the Hudson. The view just opened up over the low-lying vineyards, and they saw the sailing sloops in the bay off the Point and a steamship making its run up the Hudson toward the highlands and points north. This was Haverstraw Bay, which was the widest part of the Hudson, where it is three-and-one-half miles wide. As the light of the day was just beginning to shine, they could hear the songbirds in full song. In the distance, they could see some of the migratory birds that in a mere month or less would continue their southward flight.

This was Richard Underhill's land where he raised grapes, apples, and roses primarily for the New York City market on his 85 acres. It was a beautiful day as the sun rose, with white billowy cumulous clouds. The early morning cool air over the warm soil made the dew thick on the meadow grasses along the path and between the fruit trees. The air was sweet with the early morning breeze across the wildflowers and wild roses that grew along the paths on this end of the Point. This time in August, the apples were ripening on the trees, and so were the Catawba, Isabella, and the dark purple Senasqua grapes known to the Underhill vineyard. Elderberry, Northern Bayberry, and Beach Plum shrubs grew along the path. These shrubs were perfect for the wildlife of the area, and the fruit was eaten by many songbirds, upland game birds, and small mammals. These represented good browse species in late summer and fall, and the Underhills cultivated the native species so the animals would browse on these wild plants and not their crops. They planted many of these native species upland of and surrounding their crops. These shrubs also gave excellent cover and nesting sites for birds and attracted pollinating insects, which were also vital to the Underhill crops. In earlier times, the hollow twigs of Elderberry were used for flutes and whistles by Native Americans. The berries were also used by the locals to make good preserves, pies, and elderberry wine. The fruit of the wild rose— were especially used for jelly.

Abram stopped his horse abruptly as he noticed a yellow-crowned night heron fly low overhead toward the very southern part of Croton Point ahead of them. He sat still for a few minutes to take in the scene and the smells; he let his mind wander. "This looks beautiful right here," Abram chuntered (Yorkshire speak for "murmured"). The air breathes easy, Abram thought. Cool and crisp with the smell of wildflowers. He thought about his younger days in Sheffield, England—a dark, dank, polluted place. At times he could still smell that awful odor that came from a combination of human sewage and the pollution of England's industrial revolution period. Abram was thinking back about how badly his dad wanted to leave England for America and chase his dream. How his wife, Abram's mom, was against it, and it shattered their marriage. He was thinking how very bright his dad was and what a good choice he had made, and he was truly sorry his mom chose to stay in England while her family migrated to Croton in America. His mind drifted back to the sweet smell of late summer, and he thought that in a few months, the bay would be full of vast flocks of dark gray and white billed coot and black duck, and he thought how the winter ducks would begin to fill in the watershed's coves and marshes. Abram, his brothers, and Caleb would make another trip in a couple of months for a day of duck hunting. As his gaze went out across Croton and Haverstraw Bays, his mood turned slightly melancholy as he thought of life gone by and his mom in England. He noticed the few remaining wild roses that struggled to bloom in the late summer before their blossoms would flake off, and the beach plumbs would grow and ripen. This late in the year, many already had turned to the deep red color that meant they were ripe for picking. Abram had little time for such reflection during the long years of work at the mill and farm. His eyes caught one of the last beautiful wild rose flowers of the season being visited by a honeybee in the foreground. His eyes went back and forth, focusing on the flower and the bays beyond until his melancholy mood faded, and he lost focus on both. As he turned, he saw Caleb smiling at him. A dozen monarch butterflies, visiting the many late summer wildflowers, were fluttering just over his left shoulder.

Caleb, noticing that Abram was no longer beside him, turned and saw Abram's steady gaze out toward Haverstraw Bay. Caleb smiled; this was Abram, often caught off in some thought and far away—always thinking. "Hey, Abe. Wanna catch up?" Caleb yelled toward Abram. "We have to catch something before lunch, or we will be going home hungry, and we promised to bring fish back for the people at the meeting." The best time to fish in the late summer in the Hudson and lower Croton River was near dawn or dusk when the water temperature was lower and the insects were out. "Abe, you know that if we don't catch something in the next few hours, we are in for a hungry day." They were fishing for yellow perch, sunfish, black bass, or maybe a big catfish—the fish that inhabited the shallows of the Hudson at this time of the year. Although not their favorite eating fish, they were also hoping to catch some bluefish, and they would also set some hooks along the oyster reefs and the vegetated muddy bottoms for the juvenile oyster toadfish, which they would use for bait for other more visually enticing fish such as catfish and maybe a turtle. Although they wanted to catch enough to bring some back for the families, this was really a day for them to hang out together away from their families and constant work. A day for two best friends to hang out fishing was a simple pleasure, an interaction with nature and each other. That they would bring back food for the church meeting was another blessing.

Abram and Caleb made their way to their fishing location and tied the horses in a shady spot with lots of forage, and began to unpack the fishing gear. They did a quick, light wipe down of the horses and made sure they had plenty of freshwater. Typically, this time of the year, the river water was around 88 degrees, and today the air temperature was probably in the low 70s already. By midday, they knew it would feel like it was 100 degrees. With no recent rain, no wind, and a neap tide, they noticed the water had settled out from being its usual opaque to translucent. They watched the quiet goings-on in four feet of water—visibility being about 18–20-inches—and saw dozens of young fishes swirling up close before disappearing into the darkness and then coming back again. If this was spring, they would probably be young-of-year striped bass, American shad, and blueback herring. But this was dead summer on the Hudson. When they got to the Point, they first heard and then saw the quintessential gray-and-white Herring and the smaller Laughing Gulls. They knew they had to watch the gulls because they eat almost anything and were not above stealing their bait and the fish that they would catch.

As they spread out their gear, they noticed two wild turkey hens and a couple of poults come out of a thicket across the meadow and forage on the lawn near the edge of the brush. A few more poults and hens popped out. They counted four adult hens and a dozen poults. The poults were pecking each other and generally playing, while the adult birds kept a supervisory eye on them, intermittently pecking at the insects and grass at the edge of the meadow. As they watched the turkeys, they noticed a red fox slip into the tall brush bordering the south side; he was attracted no doubt by the hens and poults. Luckily for the poults, the fox had caught wind of Caleb and Abram and was quickly off into the deep brush; his meal was put on hold for another time.

Fishing in August can be tough, especially in unusually warm years. In warms years, the river water can get quite warm; the water in the shallows near the shore can reach into the 90-degree range. Forget fishing in those conditions. But this year was not a warm year, and there were still some fish and crabs that could be caught. Before they started their "fun fishing" with poles and bait, they walked down farther to the Point where they knew the river would be cooler and fish more prominent. This is where they would set their nets. As they walked, they noticed that the water was dotted with submerged wild celery and spiny naiad vegetation. The river at the end of the Point was ten degrees cooler and in one haul this time of the year, they expected to catch at least 20 fish or more that could include alewives, blueback herring, maybe a few early season (young-of-year) striped bass, redbreast and pumpkinseed sunfish, largemouth bass, spot tail shiners, banded killifish, and tessellated darters.

The biodiversity, biomass, vegetation, and water temperature at this part of the point was sharply different than that at their fishing hole in the sheltered cove that was mostly socked in by seaweed. They set out another net for the purpose of catching American eels, Atlantic silverside, and mummichogs. They had also planned to get some shore shrimp and fiddler crab that typically were prevalent an hour before low tide on the beachside of the marsh tide pool. Red-jointed fiddler crabs were common and could be found as far upriver in the estuary as Constitution Marsh. During past fishing trips, especially in the spring, they would occasionally catch the prehistoric-looking fish that they came to find out was called sturgeon. Sturgeons typically spawned in the Hudson for one to six years before they migrated to the ocean. These juvenile sturgeons typically congregate in March through early May in Haverstraw Bay because the combination of the soft, river-bottom sediments and the 20 feet or more depth of the water provides a perfect overwintering area for these young fish. Because it was August, they probably would not find any sturgeon in their nets today.

Spring fishing was serious. It was as important as any work they did on the farm or mill, and it was key to their families' survival. When they fished in the spring, they remained quiet for almost the entire day, with the only talk revolving around getting the job done. But this fishing trip was different. Once they set the nets, they went back to the cove to fish with their poles and enjoy the day and their friendship. As they approached the cove, Abram yelled to Caleb, who was down the bank a way, "The loser who catches the least amount of fish has to clean the fish back at the campgrounds." With no hesitation, Caleb smiled and said, "You're on." They were always competing as good friends do. Caleb knew Abram well. He knew that if he lost, Abram would clean half the fish anyway. Moreover, they knew what they did not clean their wives and friends back at camp would gladly handle.

Abram and Caleb each carried poles that were fashioned from hickory and maple saplings, split willow, and cane. Although they had some hand-carved wooden lures, plugs, and flies, they preferred to fish with minnows, worms, and insects at first and then later with some of the baitfish they caught. They would attach the bait to hooks they made from Bailey wire fashioned into different sizes. As the morning wore on, they cut a few baitfish, including squid, clams, and pieces of toadfish, and threw a few separate lines out that they would let sit to catch catfish and turtle. Their bait buckets and creels were superbly crafted wicker woven with intricate patterns using split willow stained with vegetable dyes and finished with leather bindings and straps.

They had arrived at mid-tide (which occurs every six hours). As the morning progressed, they talked endlessly as good friends can; they talked about everything, bantering and giving good-natured ribbing back and forth; this was just a time to relax and talk. Despite all the talking and the poor time of the year for fishing, they were having a successful morning. It was a beautiful August summer day on the Hudson River. The water was still as they watched the telltale signs of the tide going out. By mid-day, it was low tide, and they were looking at shallow water now. At first, as the tide went out, they saw the tiny tips of water celery starting to appear on the surface of the water. They knew that the water celery was about four feet tall, and thus they knew when they saw it, the water was about four feet deep. The green tips looked like grass swaying in the water. They noticed sand and rocks starting to appear right in front of where they were fishing. The Hudson starts around the southern tip of Manhattan. The head of the tidewater at Troy is about 153 miles, which is about half the Hudson's total length; it starts just below what later was called Lake Tear of the Clouds. Lake Tear of the Clouds is a small tarn (lake or pond) on the southwest slope of Mount Marcy, which is the highest point in the Adirondack Mountains.

Around mid-day, they took a break to have some lunch. They had already caught about ten fish between them. Abram had caught a few weakfish and porgy, and Caleb had caught a number of bluefish—all fish that are typically caught in August in the Hudson. But Caleb had also brought in a six-pound striped bass, possibly the start of the strippers coming back for their September/October migration. As they sat around sharing two of the fish they caught and a few crabs, their talk became a little more serious. They talked about their wives and kids, and Caleb began to talk about his uncle, who worked with the Bailey's, as they both agreed what a wonderful, strong person he was. All of a sudden, Abram got quiet and turned to look directly at Caleb. "You know, Caleb," Abram started, "I had a very strange dream the other night." Caleb looked back at Abram, fully attentive, because he knew Abram's mood had changed. "My dream," Abram continued, "was very murky, and all I could decipher was it had something to do with you and me.

When I woke, I had this strong feeling I could not shake, and all I could think was that we were somehow painfully connected." Abram stood and walked over to the fire and began to pour some water on it to put it out, gazing silently in deep thought. Caleb knew enough about Abram to know that when he was deep in thought, it was best to leave him alone at least for a few minutes, because he knew Abram was working something out in his mind. Suddenly, Abram turned back around, his mood visibly clearing as if he purposefully wanted to put something out of his mind, and he asked Caleb about his work, knowing his friend's passion for building boats would be a good way to change the subject. "You know, Abe, the Collyers make steam, clipper, and cargo ships as well as schooners and tugs. I really want to concentrate on making sailboats and winter ice skiffs and improve on the flat-bottomed, two-masted periauger sailing vessels that people use here to ferry goods." Abram of course, encouraged his friend and suggested he open his own shop and sell these to locals such as the Underhills, who often used these boats to ferry their products from the mill on the Croton River and the vineyards on the Point. Caleb had already made one of these for the Underhills.

"Caleb, you remember the first periauger you made for that fellow—what was his name?— Henry Warner up the river a ways?"

"Oh yes, I do, Abe," replied Caleb. "He was that wealthy New York City lawyer who bought Constitution Island up near West Point and wanted a boat to maneuver through the marsh. He had some scheme to farm wild rice there in that marsh. I wonder what happened to him?"

"I heard he lost all his money in that 1837 downturn that cost us all that business in '37 and '38," Abram answered. "My dad told me that he lives there full time in a small house with his two daughters and their aunt. He had also talked to us and the Underhills for the iron and brick he was going to use to build a summer mansion. And he had some issues with his neighbors on this side of the River. I guess they claimed they owned the marshland and wrecked some of those dams Warner built, flooding some of the rice area," Abram finished.

"Well," started Caleb, "It's a good thing I got paid before all that stuff happened."

"Too bad. He seemed like a really nice guy, and I met his two teenage daughters, Ann and Sarah when I dropped off the boat. They were staying across the way at his brother's house, who was the Chaplin at West Point." Abram added, "When he lost his money, he moved his family into the house that had thick walls built during the Revolutionary War days. He bought some materials from us to add a new wing of eight rooms."

As they headed back to fishing, Abram looked up at the sky and noticed a bald eagle circling lazily overhead, looking for prey in the water. The eagle was hoping for a fat fish that he could swoop down and catch. Abram knew that eagles frequently fish the shallows, where the smaller fish that live among the water celery are prey for the bigger fish, especially as the tide reaches its lowest. As he watched closer, he noticed that the eagle was watching an osprey. Abram had seen this before, and he knew that although eagles are among the best hunters of fish, they frequently allow osprey to do the fishing and then swoop down and steal their catch.

As Abram shifted his gaze toward the shallow water, something flashed in the sunlight, and he immediately recognized that it was a dragonfly flying among the water celery. He noticed that they were everywhere, flying low and landing on the tips of the water celery. Just then, he saw a flock of canvas back ducks swimming around the water celery further out. He watched as they alternately dove down to pull up the tasty water celery bulbs and search for insect larvae or snails, which are treats for the ducks. The tide was almost completely out now, and the water celery was lying in long ribbons on the sandy gravel. This is the best time to catch crabs, Abram thought, as they move among the celery. A little farther down the shore, he noticed a few sandpipers walking along with their funny bobbing walk no doubt looking for scud, worms, and tiny shrimp.

During the afternoon, they both caught some butterfish. These are small, rather rhombic-shaped fish lacking pelvic fins that are prevalent when the river is this warm, and the salinity is high. They were happy to catch these as they used them for bait to try to catch bluefish. With this new bait, their luck got even better, and they caught several bluefish, one more striped bass, and a few summer flounder. Just as the day was moving toward late afternoon, they had decided that they would both have one more cast, and they bet a small wager on who could bring in a fish. As Abram was reeling in his line, he felt a hard tell-tail tug and watched the line go taught; the fish was really fighting. "Oh Boy! I got a good one, Caleb." As he struggled to pull the fish in toward shore, they both caught sight of the slender and colorful spotted form.

"Oh, no!" Caleb yelled. It was a "sea trout." "You're going to lose this one, Abe". Abram knew what he meant as he now struggled to keep the line just taught enough without too much pressure as he tried to reel the fish in. This was a weakfish. The common name of this fish ("weakfish"), refers to the thin and easily torn membrane of their mouth. This, coupled with their tenacious fighting skills, make it a very difficult fish to land without the hook coming out. Abram and Caleb had fished enough over the years to know how hard it was to land these "sea trout," which was the name the locals gave to this fish. Just as Abram was about to land the fish, the fish gave one last pull, and out the hook came. "Oh well, Abe. You gave that fish a heck of a try," Caleb said as they both laughed.

It was time to break the fishing gear down and pull in the nets for the long trip to the camp meeting. They pulled the lines they had left for catfish and turtles and were lucky to find one rather large snapping turtle weighing about 20 pounds with a shell length of about thirteen inches. "Boy," said Abram at the sight of the turtle, "the Tompkins girls will know what to do with this monster. Their family has been cooking turtle from this area for a few generations, especially during the war—so I am told," he said to Caleb.

Next, they turned their attention to where they had set the nets. They had set two poles into the ground at low tide, holding up the net. They had done this many times before during the spring fishing, and they knew that as the tide moved up or down the adjacent Croton River, the fish would be pushed into the net and get caught. As they were pulling the nets, they noticed a few smaller gulls, and although they had seen these before, it was rare. These were Franklin gulls, and they were distinct from the other gulls not only by their size but by their very different coloring. These gulls were black-hooded.

When they pulled the nets, they found a fairly good haul, showing the diversity of species found in the Hudson at this time of the year. "Lucky we brought along that third pack horse," said Abram. They had decided the night before it would be needed to bring back fish for their family and friends at the meeting. The nets contained one large carp about 13 pounds as well as six-channel catfish—the larger male catfish just coming back as they typically do in August and the fall. The largest of the catfish measured 25 inches and weighed about eight pounds. The other net contained numerous eels as well as silverside and other fish. All in all, between their fishing and the nets, they had quite a load to bring back, including the one large turtle, the catfish and carp, four striped bass, numerous bluefish, weakfish that were in the nets, and porgy. Together with the blue crab, American eels, Atlantic silverside, mummichogs, and shore shrimp, they would have quite the feast for the Motts and their families and friends at the meeting—enough to share between the many Tompkins families and others.

They packed the fish in water celery and other "seaweed" that grew in the brackish water for the long truck back to the camp. As they left in the evening and started north along the river where it joins the Croton, the sunset was magnificent. It was not often that the guys stopped to enjoy, let alone think of such things. All of a sudden, while Abram gazed at the sunset, Caleb grabbed his arm to get his attention as a large white bird landed in a tree, and they noticed that there were many more, all great egrets. The light was fading fast, so their eyesight was not perfect, but they counted six at once, and four or five more were scattered about the water celery and clasping leaved pondweed. The water was also full of American waterweed, also known as Common Elodea and Coontail or Hornwort. The Hudson was not yet impacted by the invasive water chestnut, which started to invade the watershed in the late 1800s. The white birds at sunset made an amazing sight. Just as they turned their horses back to the trail, they heard a series of high-pitched whistling or piping notes as a large bald eagle flew from the river's edge back inland.

This part of the hot summer also required a lookout for thunderstorms, which often came whistling down the Hudson from the Highlands. As they set back on the trail, they heard a few peals of thunder off to the north followed by a loud, sharp crack that accompanied a lightning strike far in the distance. They could see the sky over Storm King darkening as an evening thunderstorm was brewing, and they hoped they would make it back before the storm.

CHAPTER 16

Dam Break

The Day That Changed the Croton River Valley Forever

"On January 8, 1841, a heavy snowstorm followed by days of torrential rain made the waters of the Croton swell, setting off a collapse of the incomplete and ill-designed Croton Dam and sending a wall of water and masses of ice and debris crashing through the Croton Valley for three miles to the Hudson River. The disaster took three lives and destroyed numerous houses, mills, factories, roads, and bridges. The engineers reconstructed the dam with a larger spillway but did not restore the economic life of the Croton River below the dam, which, due to flood damage, was no longer deep enough to be navigable by commercial vessels." —History of the Croton Water Works – Jerome Park reservoir and the history of the Croton Water Works

Villages—like people—are born, grow, and evolve as time passes. Events take place that influence who people become and how a village evolves or changes. The Croton Dam and aqueduct caused major changes to the Croton River Valley. They changed the history of the place and the people, and the entire background, landscape, and character of the community were altered in a major way forever.

It wasn't the first time in the Croton River Valley when a sudden rise in the level of feeder streams and the Croton River created a flood, a freshet. On the contrary, these freshets were well known; the conditions created by heavy rains combined with the rapid melting of snow and ice were known events and common in late winter-early spring in the northeast United States. And they were certainly well known in the Croton River Valley. Perhaps things would be different had the chief engineers studied the Freshet of 1818 when two separate mills operating on the lower Croton River were wiped out.

Self-taught Chief Engineer J.B. Jervis and his assistants Horatio Allen, F.B. Tower, and James Renwick were egotistical men. Their choices, lack of historical knowledge, and inaction helped to change the Croton River Valley forever. In the end, it did not matter. New York City still got its water, and that water allowed it to become one of the greatest cities of the world. The project received credit for being an engineering marvel. The fact that it altered the lives of a few people in Croton and changed the Croton River forever was of little consequence.

Perhaps it was their pompous and elite natures or their egos. Perhaps they were just not the engineers they thought they were. Maybe it was simply that the overflow weir was insufficient to discharge the water. Or more likely, it was their overarching need to quickly complete their massive project to supply water to New York City. To meet the deadlines and to soothe the Whig politicians fearful of more cholera and yellow fever outbreaks, Jervis changed the original Douglass design by moving the dam location. His ego's need to exceed expectations coupled with political pressure from the Whigs led to miss-engineering the dam in his haste to get the job done.

The fall was short in 1840 in the Hudson Highlands. Cold and snow started early and continued up until Christmas, with many days below freezing. Another large snowstorm hit just before January 1, followed by more record cold weather. The Hudson River was iced over below Sing Sing, and Croton Cove was closed by ice. Well over twenty inches of snow covered the Croton River valley.

It's common to get January thaws in the northeast. But this was no common January thaw. Dramatically rising temperatures started in early January along with several days of heavy rain totaling more than 14 inches. The melting snow and three days of heavy rain swelled the Croton River and its feeder streams. Just after midnight on January 6, the rising Croton River took Pines Bridge from its footings. With its debris crashing into the river combined with the debris of several smaller bridges, buildings, trees, brush, and large chunks of ice created a destructive force. The debris mingled with the thick, jagged ice flow toward the unfinished dam three miles below. Historical records at the time recounted the following: "At about two in the morning on the 8th, the water rose so high that it started to spill over the unfinished earthen embankment that formed part of the dam," putting the lives of the people below in grave danger.

Two miles below the dam "at the confluence of the Croton River and Hunter Brook", the Bailey brothers John, Abram, James, and Joseph stood near the western border of John's farm on the banks of the river and just west of their mill. John's house was closest to the mill, and James Sr. lived with John and his family. George Twigger, their brother-in-law, and his son, their nephew Walter, were also there. Family friend Caleb Croft and his uncle, old hand William Evans, had just walked up. The two had just returned from bringing the exhausted Bailey patriarch, 70-year-old James Sr. home.

"Uncle John," Abram asked, "did you get our father home ok?" Uncle John nodded; he was too tired to explain that they had carried the older Bailey upstairs and put him to bed. The Bailey clan and forty of their workers had just worked nonstop in the pelting rain all day on January 7 and into the night until almost 2 am Friday, January 8, erecting levees along their settlement on the river's western shore. They had worked all day in a pelting rain, hour after hour, without talking, just steady labor. They stood there soaked to the skin from the nonstop rain and the sweat from the nonstop work, and all were exhausted. Now the moon shone brightly, and a slight mist was rising from the river and valley areas as it does after a long rain. This was coupled with a fog forming because of the now clear sky and very slight wind of warmer air interacting with the remaining cold blanket of snow—an eerie combination. River smoke, some called it, is mainly caused by evaporation. This type of fog is rather shallow and generally lies low near the surface, especially close to places with large temperature differences with the air colder than the water. The river was much slower to cool down than the surrounding land. It looked like steam rising off the water, referred to by the locals as "steam fog."

The Bailey's hoped their efforts would keep the Croton River from flooding the mill, farms, and the other dwellings and structures surrounding the mill where the workers lived. The Bailey mill was an extensive establishment, and it employed about fifty men and included the mill, outbuildings, stock houses, tenant/dwelling houses, and other structures—totaling over twelve buildings in all. In ten years, the Bailey's had developed an impressive thriving enterprise.

The Bailey's knew the history of freshets; everyone in the valley did. They were desperate to protect the Bailey Wire Works and their homes. What they did not know, could not know, was that the dam being erected upstream did not match the pompous ego of its head engineer.

As they stood on the bank of the river, Abram looked at his older brother John and their brother-in-law George and asked, "What do you think?" John Bailey, like his father, was a man of few words but could also be counted on for sound thinking. "I figure the dam upstream will hold back the water, but I am worried about the river itself and how much water they let over the dam." George nodded his head in agreement and added, "I don't know what else we can do." George had his nine-year-old son, Walter, with him who was acting as a runner between various crews. Dead tired, they felt they did everything humanly possible, and they had already sent their tired workers to their homes nearby. They had little idea what approached. The Bailey's wrongly assumed that Chief engineer Jervis's men were likewise preparing the dam and areas above and below and would control the flow to avert disaster.

The Bailey's had met Jervis a few times. Jervis and his assistants had met with all the prominent families and landowners along the river before construction began and a few times during construction. In the beginning, they met to try to ease the outrage over the taking of land for the project, but as the project moved forward, they met to quell the trouble between aqueduct workers and the locals. There were other meetings with the assessors to determine what would be paid for the property and lands. The Bailey's, like most of the locals, were honest, no-nonsense people. The Croton families were a combination of some of the oldest families who settled this part of the country or were more recent settlers like the Bailey's, who came to ply their trade as manufacturers or shipbuilders. They spotted Jervis immediately as a pompous elite who looked down on them. But they thought he had to be somewhat competent given the job he had. They were not men of politics; they were men of work. As the project moved forward, the landowners, farmers, and mill owners took note of the failings of the design. They began to make fun first openly and then became more serious as they saw flaws. Jervis and his assistants had ignored their warnings and made light of these "backward folk."

At midnight, about a mile above the dam, the raging waters wrenched Pines Bridge from its foundation, dropping the bridge into the roiling water along with other small buildings, uprooted trees, and miscellaneous dikes and structures all moving swiftly toward the Croton Dam. The water was rising at almost one foot an hour. The swollen river and feeder streams kept pumping waters toward the dam, and eventually, the pent-up river flowed several feet deep over the masonry lip. Making matters worse, the final embankment was not yet built to its full extent and lacked its critical vertical protection wall.

A small group of workers at the dam was struggling to add a small dike in the dark on top of the dam's incomplete embankment, but this was far too little and far too late. They had thought that Jervis would send many workers and supplies because they had sent warnings to him days before. They thought surely by now the engineers would have sent more men from the aqueduct work to support the efforts given the weather events of the past few days. Once again, the wise men of New York City had arrogantly underestimated the needs. By midnight, the workers abandoned the effort, and by 2 am the debris from upstream had reached the dam. Realizing that the dam was going to break, one of the contractor's sons, Albert Brayton, was dispatched downstream sounding alarm horns. The poorly constructed, badly engineered, and incomplete dam was being pounded and began to fail. Just before 3 am, the water rose five feet above the dike; the river and debris swept across the top of the dam, slicing away a 200-foot earth section of the dam, and soon the entire dam-works was lost under the raging water.

Dam laborer Patrick Burke had already retired to his shanty just below the dam. He fell asleep from exhaustion and liquor. Despite the roar of the water as the embankment gave way at 3 am, he was out cold, and he was washed away. According to reports, the river smashed through Burke's shack, and his body was found the next day half-buried in a sandbank three miles downriver.

The Tompkins farm had stood along the Croton River for sixty years. As the river rushed down the valley, aged and infirm Solomon Tompkins had to be dragged from his bed by his son, who carried his father 30 feet uphill as the water, debris, and ice took the Tompkins farm.

The Bailey's heard the horns first, and as they stood just about to leave for home, a tumultuous explosion filled the valley, and the sound could be heard for miles around. Abram yelled, "Uncle John, you and Caleb go open the sluices! Joseph, go warn our families!" John yelled back at Abram, "I better go get father from the house!" Abram turned and went after Caleb. He reached Uncle John and Caleb just in time to see the raging water coming down the river. It was amazing: a wall of water and debris sweeping down the river at least 50 feet high. Uncle John, looking back at Abram, yelled, "Too late; run for high ground!" In a matter of seconds, but it was almost as if time stood still, Abram glanced to his left and saw his best friend, Caleb, with his shock of blond hair fallen across his face, wave to him, turn, and run down-river along the western dugway that curved uphill toward his home and young family. He then glanced right and saw people leaving their homes for higher ground up the steep slopes of the Croton River Valley. He saw Uncle John followed by Robert Smith, a mill worker, yelling at people to climb the trees. Uncle John and Robert Smith had stopped to help people up the trees. As the scene froze in Abram's mind, he turned to go to his family and high ground. He did not know if it was the last time he would see his friends, but he had a wife and kids to get to.

After helping the last person into a tree, Uncle John and Robert Smith began to be overtaken by the water and debris. They turned and ascended the only tree nearby—a cedar of small size, which was borne down by the water, ice, and floating timber into the current. Uncle John and Robert Smith were carried away.

The entire Bailey settlement was engulfed in the frigid, raging water and debris. The rolling-mills and wire factory situated closest to the banks of the river were instantly carried away, together with their dwelling-houses, tenant-houses, etc. They lost all their machinery, stock, furniture, goods, and more.

John Bailey met his father, James, the patriarch of the clan, at the front door holding a cashbox of gold coins. John carried his dad through the waist-deep, swirling water to higher ground, but the box and gold were lost in the process. A dozen or so desperate people, including several Bailey's, a young girl, and two mothers in soaked bedclothes clutching infants, also made high ground. So rapid was the flood that some fifteen individuals could only climb trees for safety. Among them were Mr. Joseph Bailey, his sister Mrs. Mitchell, and her son William, and a number of other women with infant children. It took several hours until the water subsided enough for rescuers to come in make-shift rafts of wood and barn doors and for the fire squads to come in open boats. Several members of the Bailey family, including Joseph and his wife and kids and several of their neighbors, were picked from trees. The last to come down was Mrs. AcRay and her infant.

Every bridge across the Croton, including Quaker Bridge, Hallmans Bridge, Woods Bridge, and Pines Bridge was washed away. Lost too were barns, stables, farmhouses, and much valuable property and supplies. The Bailey Mills was the most damaged. The wire stock, equipment, structures, and homes were all lost. Local reports described events as follows: "As it raged below the dam, the water and debris "swept everything away on the river. When it roared through the narrow Croton River Gorge, the water rose to a height of 50 feet before gushing out into the Hudson, silting out the mouth of the Croton River with mud and rocks" carrying away in its course below the Bailey's, Quaker Bridge, Holman's mills, the old piers of the old Croton Bridge, fences, timber, portions of orchards, soil, and roads along the banks of the Croton. The tons of sand and gravel and debris almost filled the estuary, formerly one of the best harbors on the Hudson River, and made the Croton River unnavigable to the sloops and schooners from that day forward.

By morning, the immediate devastation was visible. The Van Cortlandt Manner was saved when the water rose to within three feet of it and then receded. The Van Cortlandt mills were destroyed along with the Underhill and Hollman Mills. Every bridge and mill across the Croton for sixteen miles from its mouth was destroyed, including the aforementioned Quaker Bridge, Hollman's Bridge, and Pines Bridge, as well as barns, stables, and farmhouses. The Bailey and Hollman Mills was the most damaged, including the loss of stock, equipment, and homes. The only structure of the dam remaining in the river was its masonry portion. The Lounsbury, Tompkins, Purdy, Ryder, and Rowlee families put up families in their homes and provided food to the families most affected. They worked night and day with the affected families to clear away debris and salvage anything they could.

Four days later, the Bailey clan stood stoically around the Bailey plot at the Bethel Cemetery. There was James Senior in the middle, surrounded by Abram, John, James Jr., and Joseph. The Twiggers were there and the Bailey women, Clarissa, Jane, Josephine, and Ellen. Their friends and members of the community stretched back toward the church from the plot, including the oldest families from Croton, the Purdys, and the Tompkins. Caleb Croft and his young family stood next to Abram and Joseph. They were there to bury their friend and Uncle William Evans. He had lost his life-saving others, and he was James Sr.'s friend who helped start the mill from the beginning. None of the family knows the history of the two men—James Bailey Sr. and William Evans—just that their bond was strong, and James Sr. relied upon William. The Bailey's decided they would bury "Uncle John" in the family plot in a place of honor at the head of the gravesite. They had purchased a red sandstone headstone, which was popular at that time.

The Minister led the prayer:

"We commend unto thy hands of mercy, most merciful Father, the soul of this our brother William Evans departed, and we commit his body to the ground, earth to earth, ashes to ashes, dust to dust ; and we beseech thine infinite goodness to give us grace to live in thy fear and love and to die in thy favour, that when the judgement shall come which thou hast committed to thy well-beloved Son, both this our brother William and we may be found acceptable in thy sight. Grant this, O merciful Father, for the sake of Jesus Christ, our only Saviour, Mediator, and Advocate. Amen."

Abram was the spokesperson for the Bailey clan. It was left to him to speak a personal tribute to their friend. Abram started by telling the gathering of the heroic acts and how many people Uncle John saved, and what an honor it is to place William in the place of honor in the family plot.

Abram then recited the following prayer:

"The Death of Someone We Love"
"The death of someone we love and care about
Is like the death of part of us.
No one else will ever call out from within us.
Quite the same responses, the same feelings or actions or ideas.
Uncle John's death is an ending to one part of our story.
Lord, as we look back over Uncle John's life
We ask that you receive our friend.

He will continue on in our own lives.
Our love for him reminds us that our sharing.
In one another's lives brings both support and pain.
Our being parted from him reminds us of our own mortality.
And that your love is enduring.

We thank you that our love for Uncle John draws us together.
And draws us closer to his nephew Caleb and his family.
Because of him, his family is our family from now and through future generations.
And gives us a new appreciation of one another.
And of the beauty and fragility of relationships.
Which mirror your grace and goodness to us.

Hear this prayer for our love's sake.
Amen."

Then Abram finished with something he wrote that held the most meaning to him—"May their souls be bound in the Bond of Life they gave to us and to others. Life goes on. We will live it for them and the future."

Little did the gathering know that this prayer held meaning for their future and future generations, stretching through time and centuries.

After the ceremony, as they all gathered in Bethel Church, William Purdy came to Abram to offer all his and his families help. The Bailey and the Purdy families were friends even though the Purdys were Quakers. One of the oldest families, the Purdy family, settled in Cortlandt in 1735. It was William Purdy, the eldest of the Purdy sons, who rebuilt the covered wooden bridge over the Croton River at his own expense in 1830 because he wanted access to the Quaker meeting house in Croton for his friends. This bridge, too, was gone. It was Joshua Purdy, William's younger brother, who was Abram's rival for his wife Catharine's hand those many years ago. Long ago, these two had become friends.

"Abram, you know that we will do anything to support you and your family. Have you spoken to that waterman Jervis or his crew of appraisers? I don't trust those guys," said William.

Abram looked at William and said, "My father and brothers have been negotiating with these people for months, but that was before the flood took everything we own. We had not come to any agreements with them before because they way undervalued our worth. My dad came here with us in tow from England in 1831. It was his dream to leave the stench behind. We made our way to this beautiful valley and worked day and night for what we had. These Whigs and so-called engineers have taken everything from us but our will and pride. You and the rest of the Purdys have always been generous, William. We accept your kindness, and we will never forget—never."

As the group descended from the cemetery, they could see the various iceboats in the distance along the Hudson. It was a bright, sunny, cold day. The iceboats were of various forms, but most consisted of a strong wooden triangular platform placed upon three sled-runners with skate-irons on their bottoms. The rear runner was worked on a pivot or hinge by a tiller attached to a post that was passed up through the platform for steering. The boats contained sails and rigging similar to the common large sloops, and they sometimes traveled at the rate of a mile in a few minutes. Caleb had constructed a number of such boats for locals on the river, and probably some they saw were his. Life had resumed in the valley, but it would never be the same for the Bailey's.

It was a sad day in the Croton River Valley as they placed William Evans in a place of honor in the new Bailey plot just down from the Chapel. But life must start anew. The following was placed in the Hudson River Chronicle on Tuesday, January 19, 1841:

"Croton, January 11, 1841

The undersigned return their sincere thanks to their neighbors for the very liberal aid extended to them and their families after the late destruction of their works by the bursting of the Croton Dam, and they would particularly acknowledge the kindness and attention of Messrs. Henry Lounsbury, Robert Tompkins, Gabriel Purdy, Elias Purdy, William Ryder, Thomas Rowlee, and William Purdy, for the prompt and efficient aid afforded them.

Signed

      James Bailey, Sr

      John Bailey

      Abram Bailey

      James Bailey, Jr.

      Joseph Bailey"

CHAPTER 17

I Lost My Dreams in the Flood

Bailey Mills after the Flood

It all started with Burr and Hamilton and the formation of the Manhattan Water Company in 1799, and it was settled by Whig politics, fires, and disease epidemics. Hailed as one of the great engineering achievements of the 19th century, even with the need to rebuild the dam, the Croton Dam and Aqueduct project took five years. It was begun in 1837 and completed in 1842. The aqueduct carried water 41 miles from Croton, New York, to two reservoirs in Manhattan, where it was distributed to the city. The consequences of the project on the Croton River Valley were minimized in the shadow of the project and what it meant to New York City. The Whig politicians dispatched their hired experts and land assessors to finagle with farmers, mill owners, and country folk. At completion, the engineers responsible were hailed as great men and benefited greatly. Nowhere in the accolades was the story of Croton and the lives of the people the project affected. Why would there be? Their stories and the consequences were meaningless to the future of New York City. It was a small price to pay for water for the great city—water for Gotham.

"I lost my love in the flood"– The freshet was what the locals called an old fashion one. They had warned the chief engineer and the contractors responsible for building the dam. But J.B. Jervis, the self-taught railroad and canal engineer, the project's egotistical chief engineer, dismissed this information and forged ahead. He had already changed the location and design of the dam from the plans of the original engineer, D.B. Douglas. The local farmers had ridiculed the earthen part of the dam. J.B. Jervis and his contractors derided their warnings and bristled that the backward locals wouldn't know anything about such grand engineering. During the project, one of Jervis's assistants wrote to his relatives that he was tiring of the "monotonous course of life" in what he described as the "semi-civilization" of the Croton Valley. The farmers and entrepreneurs of Croton—the industrious, hardworking people of Croton, were looked down on by these pompous government "engineers." The elitist outsiders regarded the local folk as beneath them in intelligence and social status. And as usual, the opposite was true.

After the disaster, Jervis had told the commissioners in NYC that it was caused by "unprecedented rain." He barely admitted that this "setback" threw several families at the Bailey's' Mill and their laborers out of employment. Jervis did not do his required research, typically embedded in any civil engineering project. He apparently was ignorant of the Westchester Herald story published about the 1818 freshet and the great damage it caused to "two Merchant Mills owned by Gen. Cortlandt." There were later freshets that he apparently ignored or did not bother to learn about. In their desire for fame and glory, Jervis and his assistants rushed to get the dam and project completed. The beauty of the Croton Valley and the fortunes of its people were changed forever because of Jervis's hubris. Did it matter? New York City—Gotham—had its water, and the lives of a few uncultured farmers and small businessmen mattered not. These were meager enterprises, after all.

An article from the New York Herald [New York, New York] 13 Jan. 1841 explained that the disaster had thrown whole families, rich and poor, employer and employee equally, out without home or means. They were left solely reliant on the charity and hospitality of their friends and neighbors for food, raiment (clothes), and shelter. The callous miscalculations and shortsightedness of the government's engineer reduced the Bailey family from the state of wealthy capitalists giving, food, clothing, and shelter to fifty or more workers and their families to outcasts without a place of their own. Their workers' families were in the same situation.

A few years before the disaster, The Westchester Herald newspaper had made a trip to the aqueduct works and specifically the Bailey Mills on, of all days, Independence Day. At that time, the paper reported that the Croton Aqueduct foreign labor gang was nearing over 4,200 men. After touring what the reporter described as "the flourishing and extensive works of English-born James Bailey and his four sons," the reporter wrote effusively that though the Bailey's knew that the water project would destroy their current business, the Bailey's were planning on making their current and future endeavors as profitable as possible. They had plans to move their mill to another spot on the

Croton and continue operations. The reporter gushed about the Bailey's "go-ahead spirit" and wrote that they were currently negotiating the compensation due them for the impending loss of their business location. The reporter suggested that negotiations with the project appraisers would "award justice to the worthy and industrious Bailey's." The destruction of their mill changed their negotiating position. After a lengthy court battle, the Bailey's reluctantly settled for a pittance of the value of their land and enterprise. The engineers gained great prominence as the politicians' land assessors dealt their poison to the Croton families with little fanfare.

The Bailey's were not the only Croton family to lose their livelihood. The Tompkins farmstead, which had prospered for over 60 years on the river, was decimated. The house and sprawling farm and mill complex, along with all its equipment and most of its animal stock, were lost. Other mills on the river also suffered. Most notably, the Underhills' mill near the mouth of the Croton lost their half-century-old grist mill. The flood had destroyed the navigability. Even the shallow draft, flat-bottomed, two-masted periauger sailing vessels could no longer reach the Underhill Mill at the mouth of the Croton, let alone mills and farms upriver. Periaugers of varying sizes and designs were used extensively on the Hudson and Croton Rivers and were used as ferries and to transport goods to and from the towns along the river. All this ended in January 1841. Sloops and schooners were no longer able to come up the Croton. Periaugers would only later again travel the Croton after some minor dredging.

During the operations, the Bailey's kept meticulous records of the goods brought to and from the mill site as well as the names and dimensions of some of the sloops and schooners that made deliveries to the mill. Some of these were up to 75 feet in length with drafts of at least five or six feet. Because this could no longer occur in the silted in Croton, ship loading was carried out at the Croton and Sing Sing docks. The stock was shuttled to these docks to and from the rebuilt mills via the small, flat bottomed periaugers through a narrow small dredged channel. The Underhills, in particular, used custom-built periaugers. These boats worked well, and their use predated the disaster by many years. Many of the current crafts were variations of that design based on the 60-foot flat bottomed "Dread" owned by Cornelius Vanderbilt, which had sideboard or centerboard keels that allowed for their travel up the Croton River even without a deep channel as would occur when the tide was low.

J.B. Jervis and his assistants came to the disaster scene later the day of the disaster. Jervis wrote an account to the Whig commissioners in which he suggested some fault in the dam's design but blamed it all on a freak of nature. What he did not note, however, was that he had grossly under-calculated the potential flooding even though two previous floods suggested such a possibility. His arrogant tip to nature was his grossly underestimated dam design, and worse, his lack of response in the days that led up to the disaster to bolster the unfinished dam. The assessors did their dirty work, and the New York City commission totaled damages at $673,000 for all concerns to be paid out of the city's Croton funds—a sum far below what the damages really were in actual loss of equipment, supplies, livestock, homes, and future livelihoods. They never came close to the compensation for the damage to the lives lost and the future of the Croton families.

For the Bailey's in particular, the total was a joke. The Bailey's no longer had negotiating position with the appraisers, and after years of litigation, the Bailey eventually collected only about $70,000, including $20,500 for the mill houses and farm, $5,000 for stock and iron, and $22,000 for clothes, records, agricultural stock, and implements. The Bailey's believed they were in honest negotiations with the commission for a sizable sum prior to the dam break. After the dam break and the total loss of their mill, they settled for pennies on the dollar and were taken advantage of by the Whig politicians. The politics prevailed, and only the well-connected Hollman's collected anything near their due. In the end, the Bailey's collected a pittance when considering their livelihoods and all the livelihoods of the workers who relied on them. The destruction of the Bailey mill changed their futures forever, destroying what the industrious Bailey's had established over ten years and essentially destroying their business on the Croton forever because the river was forever unnavigable, preventing meaningful commerce.

The city of New York owes a great deal to Croton and to the early residents who gave their love, livelihoods, and lives so that the city of New York could reach the greatness it has. The Whigs never compensated the people of Croton even close to adequately. They took advantage of the hardworking people "for the greater good" much like politicians still do.

The Bailey Wire Mill was formerly located on the west side of the Croton River, where Hunter Brook emptied into the Croton near the western border of the town. After the flood, Abram and Joseph rebuilt the mill farther downriver.

The mills were the defining feature of the area in their time, and in total, starting with Van Cortlandt's operation for nearly 150 years. The exact history is murky. The first were grist mills owned and operated by the Van Cortlandt's. These were reportedly located at the interface between the tidal Hudson River estuary portion of the Croton River and the freshwater rapids portion of the river allowing for the power of the rapids and the convenience of the tide for loading the sloops, periaugers, and schooners. It has been reported that this mill site was leased by the Underbills from the Van Cortlandt's. Later, in 1841, the Underhill Mill was sold after the devastating collapse of the Old Croton Dam washed much of the mill downriver. It is thought that George Hecker bought this mill to start the Heckers Flour company. The Heckers brand has been around since 1843, making it one of the oldest grocery brands in the United States. This brand was started by two brothers from England: George and John Hecker. They built their first mill in Croton, where the Underhill Mill had been. George Hecker was actually the first to create a self-rising flour, and he was awarded the "First Premium" medal for outstanding advancement in food technology at the 1851 World's Fair in London. Other mills were owned by Robert Hollman (Hollman Road) and the Bailey's.

The Bailey's never fully recovered from their loss or the long, drawn-out court case and struggled for the next 28 years to resurrect their futures. But with limited funds and the river mostly unnavigable, success was fleeting, and the new mill closed in 1869. Less than ten years later, Abram died at age 71.

Still worse, another twist of historical fate was still in store for the Bailey family and the fortunes of New York City at the expense of the Croton River. Abram and Joseph's nephew, Walter Twigger, had just turned nine when he stood on the banks of the Croton with his uncles and his father George the fateful January night when the dam broke. His mother, Mary, the Bailey brothers' half-sister, had sent her son along to help save the family business. He had worked tirelessly along with his uncles and father to save the mill only to barely escape with his life up the steep slopes when the water and debris rushed toward them.

Many years later, in 1857, when he was 25, Walter married Caroline Tompkins, the niece of Abram and Joseph's wives Catherine and Phebe. Walter and Caroline Twigger had thirteen children. In another family tradition of marring sisters, Walter's sons Charles and Frederick married the Purdy sisters Julia and

Phebe of the famous local Purdy family—one of the families that so kindly helped the Bailey's in their dire need after the dam's destruction.

In 1869, Walter Twigger and his family started a grist, cider, and sawmill in what was Abram and Joseph Bailey's rolling mill. In the early 1890s, parcels 11 and 26, including the mill, were taken from Walter by the government to build the New Croton "Cornell" Dam, marking the second time the City of New York prospered at the expense of the Bailey clan. The dam was once again responsible for the end of their enterprise.

The industrious Bailey's and their ancestors' futures were changed by two government projects—both seeking water for Gotham—two of the largest and most influential projects of the time and maybe the most influential projects for the future of New York City. It's probably not an understatement to say that the Croton Dam project and Aqueduct system probably influenced New York City's future more than anything else. Without that water, the city never would have evolved into the business powerhouse it became. That it cost a few lives and disrupted the lives of families in the Croton River Valley—changing the course of this Bailey clan in America—was of little consequence to the future of New York City and the many lives saved in Manhattan.

After the 1841 disaster, the dam was redesigned to prevent another collapse. The earthen embankment was much stronger, and the main section was given an innovative s-curve profile. The new design worked, and the dam held up until it was replaced and covered by water when the New Croton "Cornell" Dam was completed in 1908.

The city of New York bought its future on the backs of some of the original settlers of Croton and essentially owes them millions. In the end, they paid out only $800,000 for the first dam and then more when they took land in eminent domain for the second. The flood affected all the families and businesses along the Croton River, including the half-century-old Underhill Mill at the mouth of the river. The flood permanently wrecked navigation of the lower Croton, clogging Croton Cove with rock, mud, and other debris and ending real navigation on the Croton River. But New York City got its water, and the dreams and plans of a few hundred inhabitants of the Croton River Valley faded behind as one of the great engineering achievements of the 19th century was completed, the project that brought life and vitality to the great city of New York. The massive freshet in early January 1841 was unique both in the time of the year and its magnitude. In the end, it was not only the event that changed the river forever; it also set a course of unique events that spanned centuries linking families in history. The peaceful, hardworking lives of the country folk have essentially been forgotten, and today water flows over the long-lost farms, homes, and flourishing enterprises of the past. The success of New York City did little to help the utter despair that met the Bailey's, Tompkins, and other families of the Croton River Valley. All they had built up in such a relatively short time, and their dreams were destroyed in the flood. One can scarcely believe the Bailey's and their enterprise were ever there.

Two massive government public works projects saved New York City for the future it holds today and tomorrow. It is impossible to know how the Bailey family would have fared had the projects never happened.

It all started with Burr and Hamilton. It all started when Burr hustled Hamilton in the water for a money deal that eventually ended the Bailey enterprises on the Croton. But it did not end there. The industrious Bailey's were not done. The future Bailey generations would make their success and failures, fortunes and lives, on the mean streets of the great city of New York and elsewhere. They are an industrious clan.

The children of Abram Bailey and Catherine Tompkins, John, Charles, Caroline, and Josephine were born in New Castle, New York, at the very extreme northern border of the town along the Croton River. In 1846, New Castle was increased to include the Bailey property. Abram's son John Bailey had six children, including Howard Bailey, born in 1861. Howard Bailey married Alida Carpenter. The Carpenters of Westchester trace back to Ezra Carpenter of Wilkshire, Wales, born in 1570. His ancestor John Carpenter the Hatter, born in 1714, moved to New Castle in 1736 as the Quakers emigrated from Long Island. The Bailey's from England married into local families. Together with the Tompkins and Carpenters, the Bailey's were part of the pioneers, patriots, politicians, and plain folk that were essential in the making of America. Howard Bailey, his brothers and sisters, their cousins, and their children dispersed into surrounding areas of Ossining, Mount Vernon, Yonkers, and other locations across America. Howard Bailey was Nick McCarthy's great grandfather.

The hard work and intelligence of generations that came after plied their trades and made their living and wealth in the great city of New York and elsewhere.

Could the success of these future generations be a result of the wealth stolen from their ancestors by the government of New York? Or, was it just a result of their genes, historical recurrence, or the repetition of patterns?

Today along the Croton River are a few residential structures along the riverbanks. Kayaks and canoes paddle up and down from the launch near the railroad bridge at the mouth of the Croton as it empties into the still magnificent Hudson. They paddle with the tide past the old Japanese tearoom structure—now a residence—that stands on a large, magnificent rock and up to the rapids that halt their advance. Just below the rapids are the remnants of the old mill raceway—a brick arch tied to the land by a neatly built massive stone wall. A tree grows atop the brick archway with its roots stretching across to the soil on either side. Just below the archway is a small boulder at the shore jutting out into the water. A thick iron bolt juts out of the boulder—a reminder of where the sloops tied off in the 1800s during the transfer of goods and products.

Chapter 18
The New Age of Rugged Individualism

The process clerk turned to her assistant and said, "They're coming out of it. I've never seen this before." The assistant nodded and said, "I know. I could not believe this when I was setting it up. Master historian Jedidiah was in shock when he gave the finished product to me. Apparently, not only was this his last case, but parts of his ancestry were embedded within it, making this truly the most unique case ever in the process. There should be an interesting response when they come back to the present. This has to be the first time this has ever happened!" Bailey opened his eyes in amazement.

My name is Jedidiah—a biblical name that traces back to an ancestor long ago. I was assigned this case, which was supposed to be my last case because I am a master historian and familiar with the geographic and historical records of Cortlandt. I am a Ph.D. geneticist with a minor in philosophy and the science of history. My main task was that of assembling portions of the detailed history for the process, adding the background that gives substance to the otherwise un-sequenced events the process spits out. The process requires trained historians with extensive knowledge of genealogy and DNA database research. How could I know, however, that parts of my own history would find their way into the process for these two boys or that the process was identical for both of them? This was truly a wonderful case with which to end my career.

It was May 4 in the year 2095, the latter part of the 21st century and infancy (95th year) of the 3rd millennium—the 95th year of the 21st century and the 6th year of the 2090s decade. Earth's civilization was just into the new Second Age of Enlightenment. It was Bailey McCarthy's 16th birthday, and he was just being revived from the voluntary pre-adult "Revelation Process." The process was not mandatory because nothing was in the new Second Age of Enlightenment. The people who started the movement, its primary directive, required individualism and individual freedom.

Bailey McCarthy went with his best friend, Croft Evans. Their names, formed by their parents, represented a combination of two ancestral names from the 19th and 20th centuries in the latter part of what was now considered the Age of Greatness. Bailey McCarthy and Croft Evans were two athletically handsome young men. Bailey had the unique trait of both the Bailey and McCarthy families, a strong chin with a deep clef and brown hair with reddish highlights, the only difference in its spiral or ribbon-like nature.

Earth's civilization had come a long way since the end of the second millennium—the tenth and final century of that millennium. It was near the end of the 20th century when the speed of things began to accelerate when Future Shock, as described by Alvin Toffler in 1970, began to affect humans, causing the rapid end of the Age of Greatness. Now in 2095, the Second Age of Enlightenment was still in its infancy since the Revolution of 2076. It did not take long for the rush to progressive socialism by the 2020s to run its course and create the predictable revolt of individuals. Human greed had its inevitable outcome. Humans, as do most species, possess a natural greediness—it's built into their DNA and is an ingredient in self-preservation. There is always a small portion of any population in which greed is virulent, reckless, and unfettered. Untrammeled human greed under a civilization run under socialism is far more devastating to the populace than greed under capitalism. Human greed under this kind of socialism always leads to totalitarianism, and that is why all societies based on virulent socialism ultimately fail and fail in devastating ways to human populations.

The Age of Greatness in this Second Age of Enlightenment was considered to consist of the latter part of the 18th century, all of the 19th century, and the early part of the 20th century. It was named the Age of Greatness because it included the original Age of Enlightenment, also known as the Age of Reason, which was predated but included the French and American revolutions, developed in the prominence of philosophy, science, and engineering, and culminated and ended in a trend toward globalization and totalitarianism. It included near its end an age where men of the greatest two generations fought aggression and fascism and survived the economic and public devastation of the great depression. Oh, the age of greatness had its flaws, some of which were despicable and truly egregious. Slavery and indentured servitude were examples. The end of the Age of Greatness would see the world become dominated by a government that prohibited opposition parties, restricted individual opposition to the government, and exercised an extremely high degree of control over public and private life. It started off small with the reduction of individual freedoms by enacting more and more regulation and government control. It was fed to the public, falsely claiming that the government would care for their every need. The preceding Age of Greatness was dominated by self-reliance, personal responsibility, self-determination, and work ethic and resulted in industrialization and growth.

The Age of Greatness was the age of individualism. It ended as government started to take control over individuals and international global governance was forming. The belief that all of Earth could be governed by a few started to take hold with the European Union, and as the age of computers and robotics commenced fully by 2019, the people had less and less work and more and more free time. To cement its power, the global government was forced to control the people more and more. This was extenuated in 2019–2020 when a worldwide pandemic spread out of China and across the globe, providing excuses and justification for governments to control the population. By the time word was surfacing in November of 2019 that a new virus was sickening and killing numerous people in one section of China, it was already too late in the global world of the early 2000s. As more and more people became sick and deaths accumulated across the globe, and as the morbidity and mortality rates rose, governments rapidly took more and more control—at first under the guise of proper public health policies.

People were sure that life had changed for good as the pandemic raged within months of the first acknowledged cases in China. As the extremely communicable illness spread and as the infectious rates rose, extreme measures were taken by governments and when predictable spikes occurred, the progressives used that as a hammer to isolate people more. In the United States, individual governors and even mayors of large municipalities such as New York City, which was the hardest hit at first, began to enforce executive orders resulting in the loss of civil liberties as the more authoritative politicians used their power to control people's lives in direct opposition to the heart of the Constitution and Bill of Rights. At its height, the government had shut down all but essential services, and people were essentially quarantined in their homes—especially in the hardest-hit locations, where cases rose rapidly. Overnight, people went from listening to rap music and "hooking up" to talking to each other in their driveways six feet apart with masks covering their noses and mouths. In some of the more authoritatively controlled areas, even this type of gathering was forbidden. Heck, people were not allowed to run by themselves in a park or go fishing, let alone congregate in their own cars for a church sermon. "Social distancing" was the term used to isolate the sick from the well and the well from the virus. It did not go unnoticed that the worst affected areas of the world included the open-border European countries that thrived on high tourism or imported labor, and these became overwhelmed with casualties. People in large cities with large populations were also hard hit. People's actions were surreal, if not somewhat necessary. It was as if the population became the main characters in the types of worldwide plague or zombie apocalypse movies that were all the rage just years before.

But, just as quickly, although not soon enough for the victims, science-led to effective therapy. Within a year, the scare was over because the virus was found to be less virulent than first thought and was susceptible to treatments. Many people had very mild cases, leading to immunity. As the pandemic progressed and scientists were armed with advanced, mature statistics, it was found that, while the number of infections was great, the mortality was not as high as feared. The original scare was downgraded as the effective treatments were followed by a vaccine. Although the global population was sufficiently spooked, life eventually moved rapidly back toward pre-virus conditions, sort of like how sports fans go back to watching their sport soon after a work stoppage ends despite their threats and promises to never watch again. Or did it? Government controls had been rapidly invoked, and socializing was governed just as rapidly and came to a halt. This did not go unnoticed by leaders around the darkening world of the powerful, global, virulently greedy elite.

It was the pandemic that followed that cemented the global governance and totalitarian control. It only took seven or so years from the pandemic of 2020 for humans to forget and revert to their social habits, and the end of the 2020s mirrored the roaring 1920s. Then a truly virulent infectious virus hit the world so rapidly that no one knows where it actually started. Some still think that it was an act of war by certain global leaders who learned the lessons of the earlier pandemic to strategize how to gain global control. People who thought that this devastating pandemic was not an outcome of nature were quickly labeled as "tin hat"-wearing conspiracy theorists and set aside as kooks by the government leaders and their media minions. Many millions of the eight billion world population died or were sickened. It did not help that only a few years earlier, the globe survived the comparatively minor pandemic. Perhaps it's easy to understand with an analogy to natural disasters. When year after year drastic super damaging hurricane warnings are made, and only weak hurricanes arrive, human nature is such that the next warnings are not as seriously believed. This played a part in the pandemic at the end of the 2020s. It was all so easily calculated and ruthlessly put in motion.

Before the pandemics, by the late 1990s and early 2000s, progressives had successfully divided America using various identity wedges and basic greed. They created a tapestry of their emotional expression and then exclaimed that their tapestry was reality. They used the tyranny of the minority to undo valued traditions with the help of colleges and universities and a willing liberal media educated in these universities. They also successfully used the court system and advocacy groups to overwhelm society while the mainstream of the population was busy working and tending to their families. This eventually led to the tyranny of the masses, and progressive groupthink began to take hold in large urban centers controlled by progressive governance.

At the time, it seemed like this happened overnight, but in reality, it was crafted for many years as progressives ran the educational system for generations as well as the media and entertainment industries. Progressives sold the message through their complete control of the media and the education system and sealed the deal when their control of the burgeoning internet social media pumped nonstop propaganda into the heart and minds of the unsuspecting masses. They sold the idea to the masses that government would make everything equal and would take from the bad rich and successful individuals and redistribute to the global masses. They falsely sold the "free stuff" culture government as the protector from birth to death. They wrote books like It Takes a Village, which downplayed the need for individual families and falsely ignored individual charity and support. Then they began eroding society by introducing bizarre concepts like gender identity and divided groups using simple identity markers—skin color, gender, age, wealth, career, and so on. The pandemics sealed the deal. The people made pliable through a few generations of education and mass media propaganda coupled with the devastation of the disease ran willingly to the government to save them.

Progressives had spent generations erasing the culture of the Age of Greatness. It came in full force by late 2015, when the messaging in the United States was that the founders of the country were really bad men because progressives removed the context of the times the founders lived in and the brilliance of what they started. It was important for progressives to completely erase the founders, much like the Spanish did with the Aztec temples—demolishing them and building their own church on top—but they first had to destroy the temple, the history, and culture. Along the way, they found it also necessary to destroy masculinity, families, work ethic, and family culture by emasculating groups and forming diverse communities that could be played against each other. They are divided by gender, ethnicity, culture, or any category that would create a wedge between people. They used the tyranny of these minority groups to split the culture right down to gender identity. They purposefully emasculated the males and "masculated" the females. Then they sold government almost like a pusher sells drugs—installing governed programs that doled out "free stuff" crumbs whenever the people needed their fix. There was never a chance for real advancement, real freedom, or real growth because the government-controlled all that. Individual freedom and success were lost as more and more the society relied on the government for all its needs. The government became their perpetual mommy and daddy from birth to death. As the 2000s pushed on into the 2040s, with the help of the killer pandemics, the global government became more and more totalitarian as the need to control the masses increased and individual localities—towns and villages across the world—became more like dystopian annexes of the larger global government.

One such dystopian annex existed in the Croton River Valley and the surrounding towns that made up Cortlandt. The ancestors of the original freeholder settlers began to fight back, first through small meetings and underground Freeholder society writings. In the end, the end of this global progressive world order came down to what could not be controlled—the natural order of things; that things always revert to entropy. The Croton Valley annex had revolted, and this revolt spread quickly across America. Things always revert to lack of order and work toward unpredictability and gradually decline into disorder unless something binds them. The brilliance of the Age of Greatness and in particular, America was the belief that individual freedom within the republic held that bond. The fallacy of socialism is that it removes individual freedom and eventually requires totalitarianism to control the masses. America did not realize how very fragile their gift was until it was too late.

The global progressive rule ended relatively as fast as it started because these elitists forgot that humans are basically tribal and eventually will revolt against this authority to gain self-control. The natural greed of the individual would take over. The revolution movement started in New York State of all places in the small town of Croton, just 40 miles north of New York City. It started in a place that was once the very hotbed of progressivism. The progressive movement in Croton probably started in the early 1900s as an artistic enclave, and as time went on, the area began attracting artists, actors, and writers from Greenwich Village. During the 1920s, old farms were transformed into collectives for writers and artists, and the area became known as "Greenwich Village on the Hudson." By the 1930s, "intellectuals" and left-wing activists with socialist leanings populated the Mount Airy Road area of Croton, and it became known as "Red Hill." The area was populated by a mixture of communists and socialists. The community published a pamphlet called The Masses, which became a popular monthly journal for socialist art and commentary.

But this place, Croton, also had a previous history of rugged individualism during the Age of Greatness, and the genetics of the people that originally populated the area—the Van Cortlandt's, the Underhills, The Van Tassels, the Jays, the Purdys, the Ryders and Rowlees, the Meads and the Tompkins and Bailey's—from the Dutch, English, Welsh, and French Huguenot heritage as well as those ancestors of the black freemen and slaves from the First Rhode Island Regiment, still pulsed in its inhabitants. They were freeholders.

By the 2070s, the Croton River Valley was still relatively sparsely populated, and a few of the lands from the original freeholder farmsteads were isolated in the steep hills and rugged country. It was here that the inhabitants quietly met to discuss their small but growing movement. It had started innocently when a few members with original family heritages began to uncover their roots and history as part of the movement toward mass DNA testing, genealogy, and family history started as a fad in the early 2000s. The mass loss of life during the pandemics of the 2020's only heightened the interest in the genealogy of families. The small group of Croton families called their group the "Freeholder Society." The advancement in genetic genealogy, which matched family history and DNA markers, helped speed up the knowledge of family heritage. When this information was viewed together with the theory of Historic Recurrence or the repetition of patterns, a new world of family history opened, and links to the past as well as "genealogic" heritage and personality traits emerged.

By the time Bailey and Croft elected to engage in the "Revelation Process," the Croton area had grown into the center of the movement. The "Revelation Process" was relatively new and was initiated ten years before, around 2085. It was a direct result of the research that was done for an organic method to deprogram the population from the years of progressive globalized socialism that started not so innocently as early as the 1890s but progressed fully with the New Deal programs of the late 1930s. This progressive movement started to gain traction in the heart of rugged individualism, the United States but was advanced in Europe under European socialism. Progressive socialism started to take flight in the United States in the 1960s as progressives took control of primary schools and colleges. It caught momentum in the 2000s when progressives had control of most of the messaging, including the media, entertainment, sports, and most importantly, education and the new giant social media. The progressives used these messaging vehicles to "educate," propagandize, and program the masses into progressive global socialism.

RUGGED INDIVIDUALISM is a good way to describe the nature of the industrious Bailey's and the other families of the Croton River Valley during the height of the Age of Greatness and, to a lesser degree Nick McCarthy and Scott Croft near its end. They possessed the innate qualities of the puritan work ethic. It was in their genes and practiced by their families and ancestors. Their ancestors affirmed the doctrine of diligence in one's work. During the time of the Bailey's in the 19th century, the concept had religious overtones, and those who demonstrated hard work unto the glory of God were seen as bearing "fruit" and thus were truly saved, and those who displayed idleness were often considered damned. The Puritan work ethic emphasized work as a natural part of life, as something that could be enjoyed and something that pleased God if conducted with the right attitude. Hard work in secular life came to be seen as a spiritual act of worship. The Bailey's of the 1830s and 1840s especially emphasized this type of work ethic, and it was still very much alive in Nick and Scott in the 1960s and 1970s, although not in a spiritual/religious way. They had just viewed it as the correct way to live and conduct yourself, and their personalities driven by their genes and enhanced by their family upbringing meant that they were prideful, respectful, and self-reliant. Did Eternal Recurrence also play a role? Did the energy and matter of the Bailey's transform to the 1960s? Was it recurring again? The infinite cycle re-emerging as it transferred from the previous ancestors of the Bailey's, Clays, Carpenters, Evans, and Tompkins—the knights and coal barons and freeholders. It is said that courage sometimes skips a generation or two. It did not appear to skip any generations of the Bailey's and Crofts.

But by the end of the 1960s, progressives had made many inroads into the culture that rapidly accelerated through generations of progressive education taught from elementary school through college. During the "progressive" era, many had sold to the population the idea that the value of the puritan work ethic was a myth—that hard work was not the main factor in producing material wealth and that hard work was not character building or morally good. The idea that "idle hands are the devil's workshop" was laughed at as antiquated as free time was becoming more plentiful. By the 2000s, government was becoming more in control of people's lives. Computers and robotics were relieving man of much of the work, and more and more idle time and socialization were occurring. So too was the increased use of mind-altering and addictive drugs. Something was needed for the idle time, and the government searched for more and more ways to control the population. The youth, mostly males, were spending large amounts of time in computer gaming, which became an outlet for their masculinity as they had no outlet in society for their natural biological drive. The generation of the late 1990s and 2000s were taught in school by progressive teachers, and they were all exposed to social media, which progressively propagandized the unknowing population. The pandemics gave the global progressive governments the chance to take control of the devastated and panicked population.

The antithesis of the Age of Greatness, The Age of the Global Progressive Government, had its downfall for the same reason it succeeds. What constituted American exceptionalism during the Age of Greatness is complicated and multifaceted. Timing, location, and natural resources all played a role. Yet there was something else. It was the unique system that created a government wrapped around individual freedom and liberty. It was founded on the belief that you could make your own success and that everyone had an opportunity for self-governance. For freedom and liberty to succeed, the government would have to have a limited role. As the progressive global government took more and more freedom and liberty to control the masses, it became more totalitarian. This, in the end, was the demise of the Progressive Global Movement, which ended abruptly with the New Revolution of 2076.

Bringing back individuality—the power over one's own life—was the purpose of the "Revelation Process." It was meant to jumpstart what was already inherently in their genes—to remove the self-doubt and group think that years of progressive teaching had instilled into people, especially boys. The masculinity of their gender was long ago trampled on by progressive elites to gain power. They invented the term toxic masculinity to neuter males in society. This did great harm to both men and women, as well as the inherent nature of biology. This and other nonsense of the progressive movement had to be undone, and one method was the Revelation Process: reliving through their inherited DNA the story of their family's individuality during the First Age of Enlightenment that made their ancestors great and allowed them to strive for great things. The Revelation Process was used to kickstart the new Second Age of Enlightenment and an age of hard work and rugged individualism.

The Revolution of 2076, much like the American and French Revolutions, was the result of far-reaching social and political upheaval inspired by the need to escape the shackles of global socialism triggering the global decline of the elite progressive power structure of the global government and the elite politicians that ran the world. Individualism was making a comeback, and the need to accelerate that was the theory behind the use of the Revelation Process.

It started innocently, or so the progressives thought, through genealogy. Genealogy and the need to understand ancestral roots began to become more prevalent in the 1940s and 1950s and progressed in popularity through the end of the 20th century as people had more time to contemplate their ancestral past. A hobby of sorts by many, a growing database of ancestral information was ensured when the use of computers and later the internet took hold.

Starting around 1985, DNA testing for crime investigations was becoming commonplace, and by the end of the century, testing became more refined and common. In the early 2000s, for-profit genealogy companies started massing billions of historical records and millions of DNA data sets. Then they began to couple genetic genealogy with family relativity. Methodology grew from there rapidly, and by the year 2025, the ancestral history and DNA mapping of most of the global population were almost 95% complete as DNA testing was mandated at a point by progressives as yet another way of controlling the populace under a phony cultural diversity meme. What resulted was the opposite—the unintended consequences is what led to their undoing. With the use of historical records, most people could trace their ancestry back hundreds of years—certainly into the 18th and 17th centuries—and many well back from there. Humanity could trace its history back to origination.

At first, in the mid to late 1900s, the fixation was on social standing, racial purity, and a need for people to have a sense of ethnic belonging. This gave way in the late 1900s and early 2000s to embrace ethnic heritage diversity. The progressive movement helped foster this in the early days as a way to defend their need to divide people and their sham of government control through cultural diversity. Like many progressive initiatives, this eventually led to quite the opposite. By the 2050s, it started on a small scale within what was left of family units—a need to demonstrate kinship and pedigrees. The massive database of ancestral lineages existed. As this database was used by more and more individuals, the need for family rose and the start of the revolution began in this innocent way. The need to carve out a place for one's family in the larger historical picture, a sense of individuality, and the need to preserve family, rapidly overtook the progressive movement. The global progressive government tried to fight it by banning the use of DNA and genealogy, but it was too late. Like a wildfire, it morphed into a larger movement of individualism—the study of families and their lineage created a need for individualism. This was true diversity in the form of individualism.

The Revelation Process used the massive database to create the ancestral histories of families infinite detail, jumpstarting the innate need of the people to find their individuality through their direct family history. Much of the focus naturally tended toward the era of the First Age of Enlightenment.

Emerging from the Revelation Process, both Bailey and Croft had now relived the lives of their ancestors back in the day when their families were at both the height and nearing the decline of that individualism that made them great. Their emersion resulted in its intent—to advance their natural aggressive, confident nature that was weaned out of males and to some degree females beginning in the late 20th century because it did not meld with government conformance and need. As they merged in the hall after leaving their separate Revelation Process rooms, they gazed at each other with the realization that their lives had been intertwined for centuries. Going into the Revelation Process, they did not know that this was the first time in the history of the young process that two individuals showed up simultaneously and were given the same identical revelation.

The Revolution of 2076 was natural flux. It was the innate need of human biology. The need of humans to take back control of their own destiny and take it away from the forces that had herded them into a global family intent on controlling their behavior for the power and control of the few global elite.

As Bailey and Croft walked out after the Revelation Process, Bailey peered out across Croton Bay and the Hudson. He watched as a slight breeze off the River ruffled Croft's hair as Croft struggled to keep his light brownish-red, almost strawberry-blond locks out of his eyes. He looked past Croft to a stretch of wild rugose roses just off the shoreline. "This looks beautiful right here," Bailey murmured. The air breathes easy, he thought. Cool, crisp, with the smell of wildflowers. He was deep in thought as he walked past Croft and towards the shoreline. He was thinking about this place where his ancestors had lived, worked, played, and died. Beyond the specific family history, the Revelation Process also included the background of the First Age of Greatness and the French and American Revolutions.

Even more meaningful to the area of his ancestors was that key historical occurrences occurred in the same place of his ancestors. He thought about the great men and women who had lived and shed their blood and tears in this beautiful place. One of his direct ancestors, Howard Bailey's son, George Eldridge Bailey, was the grandfather of Nick McCarthy. Nick was the ancestor of Bailey. As he thought about what he had just learned, he became a little melancholy as his eyes focused on a beautiful rugosa rose flower. He focused on the vibrant deep red surrounding a yellow inner core of the flower in the foreground briefly before refocusing back on the ships in the bay in the background. His eyes drifted back and forth, focusing on the flower and the bay until his melancholy mood eased, and he lost focus on both. He looked out over the bay and was struck at how the shoreline was choked with dense mats of rooted water chestnuts. He recalled from the Revelation Process about Caleb's and Abram's fishing trip that might have occurred at this very spot. As his view caught the thick growth of phragmites near the mouth of the Croton River he realized that these species and especially the water chestnuts did not invade the Hudson until the mid to late 1800s and would not have been present in the Hudson during his Bailey ancestors time.

He was deep in thought, again, his light brown muscular skin glistening in beads of sweat as he pondered what had happened to his family since the time of his ancestors during the age of greatness. He thought about how the pandemic had taken his grandfather's first wife and how he married his grandmother, who was ten years younger. She was recently off the boat from the African continent as populations were easily shifting to fill the globe after the pandemic. They had met near the end of the pandemic innocently in a meeting of scientists. Bailey's granddad had Maters in Public Health from Yale University School of Medicine, and his focus had been on infectious diseases and environmental health. His grandmother was working for the World Health Organization who brought leaders in science from around the globe to pick up the pieces as the pandemic eased. They met, fell in love, and truly loved each other. Bailey thought how his rugged physical appearance and ancestral traits were a perfect reflection of his parents, grandparents, and his ancestors. As he turned his glance back, he saw Croft smiling at him, and he was brought back to the present.

"At what point then is the approach of danger to be expected? I answer, if it ever reaches us, it must spring up amongst us. It cannot come from abroad. If destruction be our lot, we must ourselves be its author and finisher. As a nation of freemen, we must live through all time or die by suicide. Abraham Lincoln"

Things have a habit of repeating themselves. Maybe it's part of the universe; it seems to happen too often to be coincidence. Some call it Historic Recurrence or the repetition of patterns. It has its own doctrine—the Doctrine of Eternal Recurrence, "The theory that existence recurs in an infinite cycle as energy and matter transform over time." Nietzsche connected this concept to many things. Perhaps when it comes to personality, human behavior, and family, the theory can be tied to ancestry and to heredity. But does it override changing culture?

Sources/References

Descendants of John Tompkins Four Centuries of Pioneers, Patriots, Politicians and Plain Folk. Compiled by Scott Tompkins and Christopher Tompkins; January 31, 2003. Note, most of the history of the Tompkins family and the Story of the Motts was obtained directly from this document.

Christopher Tompkins –" *The Croton Dams and Aqueduct*"; Arcadia Publications 10-30-2000

American Ancestry: Giving the Name and Descent, in the Male Line, of Americans Whose Ancestors Settled in the United States Previous to the Declaration of Independence, A.D. 1776, Volumes 1-2 (pages 132 & 133)

Marc Cheshire - Village Historian of Croton-on-Hudson
Charles Radke - Yorktown Historical Society
Adele C. Hobby - Assistant Curator, The Yorktown Museum
Patrick Raftery, Librarian – Westchester History

John Thomas Scarf – *"History of Westchester County: New York, Including Morrisania ...*, Volume 2"

> Westchester History

Croton History organization – Croton Resources – *crotonresources.org* – *https://crotonhistory.org/resources*

A History of the County of Westchester, from its First Settlement to the Present Time by Robert Bolton. New York, printed by A. S. Gould, 1848.

Volume 1
    Pages 115–116, 108–109, 111, 112, 268
Volume 2
    Pages 115, 139 and 195–397

The History of the Several Towns, Manors, and Patents of the County of Westchester, from its First Settlement to the Present Time by Robert Bolton. New York, C. F. Roper, 1881.

        Volume 1
        Volume 2

History of Westchester County, New York, from its Earliest Settlement to the Year 1900 by Frederic Shonnard and W. W. Spooner. New York, New York History Co., 1900.

History of Westchester County, New York, Including Morrisania, Kings Bridge, and West Farms, which have been Annexed to New York City by J. Thomas Scharf. Philadelphia, L. E. Preston & co., 1886.

> Volume 1
> Volume 2

Westchester County During the American Revolution, 1775–1783 by Otto Hufeland. White Plains, N. Y., Westchester County Historical Society, 1926. Due to copyright restrictions only limited searching is available online here.

Westchester County, New York, During the American Revolution by Henry Barton Dawson. Morrisania, New York City, 1886.

Westchester County and Its People by Ernest Freeland Griffin, editor. New York, Lewis Historical Pub. Co., Inc., 1946.

> Volume 1
> Volume 2
> Volume 3

History of the Croton Water Works – Jerome Park reservoir and the history of the Croton Water Works
http://www.lehman.cuny.edu/lehman/preservationreport/history.html

Report of Cases Argued & Determined In Supreme Court and in the Court for Corrections of Errors of New York State. by Hiram Denio. Vollume II. New York: Bank & Brothers Law Publishers, 1863

History of Westchester County N.Y. Morrisania, Kings Bridge & West Farms. by J. Thomas Scharf, AM, UD. Volume II Philadelphia: L.E. Presten & Co 1886
https://www.ossining.org/crotonriver.htm#mills

Courtesy Historic Hudson Valley, Tarrytown

Black Rock Historical Society, 1902 Niagara Street -Ms Mary Ann Kedron

The Old Black Rock Ferry Read before the Society, December 14, 1863. by Charles D. Norton. From the nineteenth century publications of the predecessor of the Buffalo and Erie County Historical Society

Pioneer Roads and Experiences of Travelers ...
By Archer Butler Hulbert, James Hall, Thomas Wallcut, Timothy Bigelow, Francis Whiting Halsey, Charles Dickens, Sir Charles Augustus Murray
https://books.google.com/books?id=a71pj9gURHYC&pg=PA95&dq=Mowhawk+Turnpike&source=gbs_toc_r&hl=en#v=onepage&q=Mowhawk%20Turnpike&f=false

Water for Gotham by Gerard T. Koeppel. Princeton University Press. 2000

"How a Massive Public Works Project Saved a Parched New York". By Sam Roberts New York Times Dec. 4, 2017
https://www.nytimes.com/2017/12/04/nyregion/croton-aqueduct-burr-hamilton.html

"The Contentious History of Supplying Water to Manhattan" Tuesday, July 16, 2013 byLauren Robinson - Museum of the City of New York
https://www.mcny.org/story/contentious-history-supplying-water-manhattan

The Water-Supply of The City Of New York. 1658-1895
by Edward Wegmann, New York: John WIley & Sons. 1896.

"The History of the New Croton Dam" by Mary Josephine D'Alvia, Published by the author; January 1, 1976

Acknowledgments

I wish to thank the following persons:

Mom and Dad – John C Gorton and Blanche Gorton (Bailey)

Brothers John and Robert Gorton

My daughter Karlee Lewis & my son Dustin Gorton

My wife Susan Gorton (Lewis) who lost a hard-fought battle against
cancer in 2012.

My Grandparents George and Alice Bailey and John (jack) and Agnes Gorton

Robert Gates who provided much of the Bailey genealogical work

Bailey Family – Ridge, Kevin, Lisa, Meghan, Sean their kids
(the legacy goes on)

Louise Magner (Bailey) & Edward Magner

Kathy Mason (Magner)

Bert and Johanne Kelly

Best friend Craig Telfer and his girlfriend Patty Foley

My high school sweetheart Madeleine Daniele

Business partner Jason Brydges

Mr. Akos Seres

Mr. Barry Booker

Mr. Carmine Tronolone

Christopher Tompkins –" The Croton Dams and Aqueduct"

Christopher and Scott Tompkins – Much of the genealogical history of the
Tompkins, Bailey's, Twiggers and Motts story came from his work

Marc Cheshire - Village Historian of Croton-on-Hudson

Charles Radke - Yorktown Historical Society

Adele C. Hobby - Assistant Curator, The Yorktown Museum

Patrick Raftery, Librarian – Westchester History

Julia Lavarnway – editor

Mary Ann Kedron – President - The Black Rock Riverside Alliance
(BRRAlliance, Inc.)

About the Author

Peter Gorton is a co-owner of Brydges Engineering in the Environment and Energy - an environmental engineering and remediation firm located in Buffalo, New York. Born in Yonkers and raised in Peekskill, New York, he received a BS degree in Public Health/Environmental Science from the University of Massachusetts and a Master's degree in Public Health (MPH) from Yale School of Medicine, where he studied epidemiology, infectious diseases, and environmental health.

Peter's 40-year career started in the infancy of the hazardous waste site assessment/ remediation and chemical/oil spill response industry and included projects across the US and military bases in the pacific. He has authored hundreds of technical, environmental investigation, and assessment reports and has been involved in over ten chemical and oil spill responses at various locations across the country.

Other academic/ business publications include "Environmental Forensics for Cost Recovery at Petroleum Contaminated Sites" for the NYS Bar Association, "Microbiological Standards for Potentially Hazardous Foods" and he was a contributing Author for "Health & Safety for Museum Professionals – 2010 Society for the Preservation of Natural History Collections.

Mr. Gorton has spent a career reviewing the history of people, places, and events. He played five sports in High School and wrestled in college. Today he is an avid kayaker.